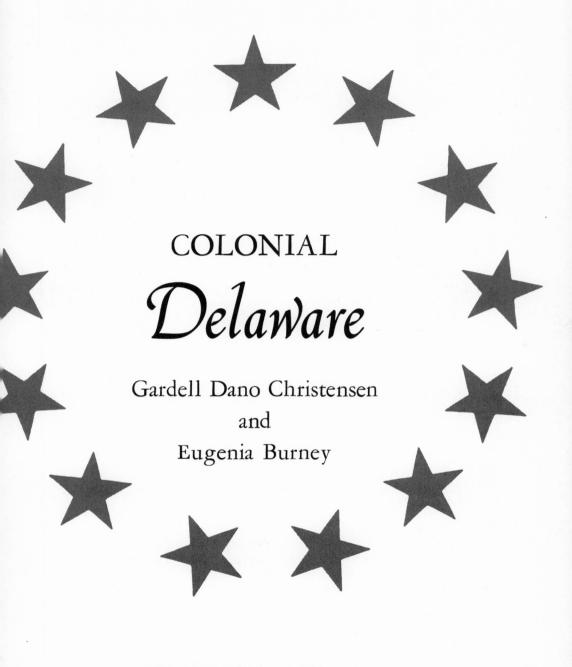

COLONIAL

Delaware

Gardell Dano Christensen
and
Eugenia Burney

THOMAS NELSON INC.
Nashville / Camden / New York

Photographs courtesy of the Historical Society of Delaware, with the exception of the following: pp. 8, 44, 79, 85, 90, 94, 120, 127, 133, 148, Eleutherian Mills Historical Library; pp. 86, 89, Hagley Museum, Wilmington, Delaware; pp. 96, 99, the Historical Society of Pennsylvania; p. 66, Mr. Dudley C. Lunt, from his book *The Bounds of Delaware*. Permission is gratefully acknowledged.

First edition

Library of Congress Cataloging in Publication Data

Christensen, Gardell Dano.
  Colonial Delaware.

  (Colonial histories)
  Bibliography: p.
  SUMMARY: Traces the history of Delaware from its discovery and first settlement to its role in the Revolution and ratification of the Constitution.
  1. Delaware—History—Colonial period, ca. 1600–1775—Juvenile literature. 2. Delaware—History—Revolution, 1775–1783—Juvenile literature. [1. Delaware—History—Colonial period, ca. 1600–1775. 2. Delaware—History—Revolution, 1775–1783]. I. Burney, Eugenia, joint author. II. Title.
  F167.C48   975.1'02   74–10265
  ISBN 0–8407–7118–5

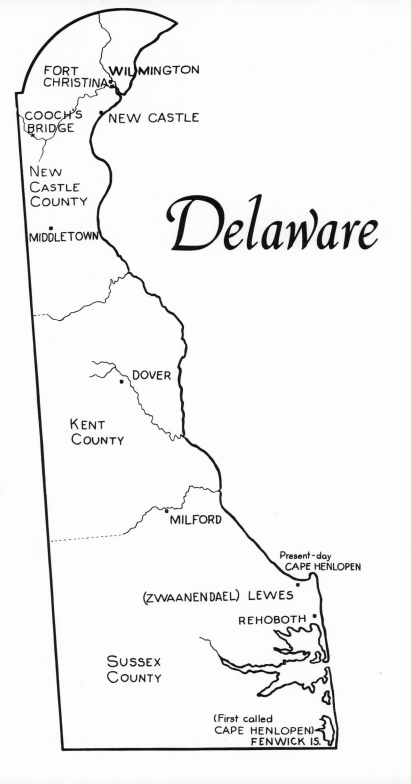

FORT CHRISTINA

WILMINGTON

COOCH'S BRIDGE

NEW CASTLE

New Castle County

MIDDLETOWN

Delaware

DOVER

Kent County

MILFORD

Present-day CAPE HENLOPEN

(ZWAANENDAEL) LEWES

REHOBOTH

Sussex County

(First called CAPE HENLOPEN) FENWICK IS.

Contents

"Delaware Indian family," a drawing by John Campanius.

CHAPTER ONE

A Changing World

The two Leni-Lenape Indian boys crouched motionless behind the bushes on the bank of the river which their people called the Fishing River (now the Brandywine) and which emptied into a broad, sluggish estuary that would come to be named the Delaware. The boys were watching a family of Canada geese paddle about in the water. Every year these same two geese returned to a little island in the Fishing River. They made a nest, hatched out their goslings, and taught them to swim and feed in the stream. For four years the Indian boys had watched the geese come back to the island and nest. The braves of their tribe shot other geese and ducks for food, but this pair was the boys' secret.

After the snow melted and the marshes began to turn green each spring, the great birds arrived, coming by the millions from their wintering grounds far to the south. The peninsula on which the Leni-Lenape lived was one of the feeding places on the great flyway for ducks, swans, and geese. For two moons they flew in over the rivers, making the sky black as if a cloud had covered the sun, and their wings made a noise like thunder. When they settled on the marshes and shallow estuaries of the great river to rest and feed, the air was so filled with their noise that the Indian boys had to shout into each other's ears to be heard.

The boys left the geese and walked along the game trail up the bank of the Fishing River, past mossy rocks, through blooming laurel and dogwood shaded by thick trees. The water roared over huge boulders on its way to join the larger, slower-flowing river. Despite the rushing water and the rocks, the great shad swam upstream, fighting against the swift-moving current to gain their spawning grounds in fresh water. Leaping over the rocks also were the great sturgeon, some of them weighing as much as three hundred pounds.

The boys paused to watch a large black bear, poised on a rock beside the river. Suddenly he darted into the water and snatched up a two-foot shad, which he carried wiggling into the bushes to eat. The Indians were accustomed to seeing bear fishing in the river, but they took a higher trail and circled around so as not to disturb this one.

The Fish Kill

A little farther upstream the two Leni-Lenape boys came upon their goal, a spot where many years ago the braves of their tribe had rolled big rocks across a narrow gorge in the river to form a V-shaped dam. (Remains of this dam are still visible on the Brandywine.) The angle of the V was downstream and was left open at the bottom. Two naked braves stood on either side of the opening with their forked spears poised over the foaming water. Other men and women splashed about on the slippery rocks along the arms of the V. They held fish brooms made of branching saplings tied together at the end to make crude nets.

Suddenly, a wave of shad came up the river, and the Indians went to work. They swept the fish out of the water with the fish brooms and tossed them onto the shore. The two men at the open end of the V darted their spears in and out of the water, bringing up a flapping

The Leni-Lenape Indians made arrowheads, axes, cooking pots, pottery baskets, animal traps, and fish weirs. This stone mortar is used as a bird bath in this Wilmington garden.

shad nearly every time. Squaws nearby held nets made of hemp, into which the fish were dropped.

Above the crude dam the children of the tribe shrieked in glee as they milled about in the water. The two boys immediately joined them in their sport, and soon all of the baskets were filled with the silvery fish. Some of the boys dragged along fish threaded through the gills on grape-vine cords.

When they reached their camp, the squaws cooked the shad by boiling them in pots over the fire. They ate all of the big fish except the backbone and head, throwing the leavings to their wolflike dogs.

The Walum Olum

The peninsula on which the Leni-Lenape Indians lived was formed millions of years ago. At the end of the Ice Age, however, about twelve thousand years ago, when the glaciers melted, the ocean rose and spread over the low coastal valleys. Only the hills remained above sea level, and the land was surrounded on three sides by water, leaving only a tiny neck connecting it to the mainland between the Delaware and Susquehanna rivers. Today the highest point of land in Delaware is only 450 feet above sea level. This peninsula is now called Delmarva for the three states that comprise it—*Del*aware, *Mar*yland, and *V*irgin*ia*.

The Leni-Lenape were a tribe of the Algonkian nation, and they were a peaceful people. The peninsula between the two great rivers where they lived gave them such security that they could usually afford to avoid war. More warlike tribes called them the Old Women or, because of their ancient lineage, the Grandfathers. When white settlement forced them to retreat from their homeland, they became vassals of the powerful Iroquois, who offered them protection for a further while. Later, of course, they were forced to move again.

The Leni-Lenape have a tribal legend of their arrival in Delmarva. Their history book consists of a group of sticks with the story painted on them in pictures. This history they called the *Walum Olum*. It tells how the Leni-Lenape came east from somewhere west of the Mississippi River. When they reached what is now Pennsylvania, they fought

9

a fierce battle with some Indians who already lived there, called the Tallegwi. From there some of the tribes went north, where they became the Iroquois. Others went east to the seacoast and became the Algonkians, of which the Leni-Lenape were a tribe. Others went south. On the peninsula between the two large bays, the tribes became known by such names as Accomack, Accohannock, Pocomoke, Assateague, Nanticoke, and Choptank. They called the great river which formed the east bay Chickohocki. Archaeological evidence seems to establish the fact that they were the first human beings to live on the peninsula.

Each tribe developed its own customs but still spoke the original language. They built villages or towns on the banks of the rivers and streams. Each village had a leader, sometimes a woman, and a council of advisers who decided when they would go to war. The men furnished protection and hunted for food. The women made the clothing, cooked the food, watched the crops, and taught the children. They made arrowheads, axes, cooking pots, pottery baskets, animal traps, and fish weirs. At their ceremonies they smoked tobacco in pipes. They planted corn by putting a dead fish in each hill to fertilize it. When it was gathered, they cut the grains from the cobs and stored them in granaries dug in the ground.

Giovanni da Verrazano

The first white man to have entered what is now Delaware Bay was Giovanni da Verrazano. Although he was an Italian, Verrazano went to France as a navigator early in 1508, and in 1523 King Francis I granted him a commission to explore the New World. Late that year, he sailed in the ship *Dauphine* as commander of the first French expedition to visit America.

Verrazano was a great letter writer, and two of his letters have been preserved. In one of them to the king, he tells how he reached a new country, never before seen by anyone, either in ancient or modern times. From his description of the latitudes, he must have sighted America first in March 1524, near the site of Wilmington, North Carolina.

Sailing slowly up the coast, Verrazano wrote a detailed description of the land and its people. When he described the great bays of present-

"Giovanni da Verrazano"

day Delaware, he romanced a trifle: "An isthmus a mile in width and about 200 long, in which, from the ship, was seen the oriental sea between the west and north. Which is the one, without doubt, which goes about the extremity of India, China and Cathay." He thought that the Pacific Ocean invaded the American continent and joined the Atlantic Ocean.

After sailing as far north as Nova Scotia and Newfoundland, which had been discovered by the Cabots twenty-seven years earlier, Verrazano returned to France. Now, France, England, and Spain all had claims to the New World.

CHAPTER TWO

The Ambitious Dutch

The first industry in America was fishing. When European fishermen heard John Cabot's report in 1497 that the ocean near Newfoundland was swarming with fish, which could be taken not only with the net but in baskets let down with a stone, hearty French seafarers lost no time in sailing to this new fishing ground. The Grand Banks of Newfoundland were fished regularly by French fishermen for sixty-five years before the first colony was founded in North America at St. Augustine, Florida, in the name of Spain.

Another forty-two years passed before John Smith arrived with a little band of colonists from England and settled at Jamestown, Virginia, May 13, 1607. Because of the explorations of John and Sebastian Cabot, England claimed the coast of North America from latitude 34 to 45 degrees north, an area from what is now the southern part of North Carolina to central Maine. The whole claim was named Virginia, but was divided into South Virginia and North Virginia, which was later renamed New England. Each section was to be settled by a different company. The London Company sent 105 settlers, one of them John Smith, to make a settlement between latitude 34 and 38 degrees north, and they settled at Jamestown.

As a colonial leader, John Smith had his ups and downs. In 1608 he grew so disgusted with his lazy colonists that he took an open boat and a few men and left the colony to its own devices while he explored the waterways to the north. In three months he traveled one thousand miles, exploring the Chesapeake Bay and perhaps entering the Delaware Bay. He made a map of the shoreline that was later printed in England.

Henry Hudson Explores the Delaware River

While Spain, England, France, and Portugal searched the newly discovered land for gold, the governors of Holland had a different idea —trade. For several years Dutch ships had brought the wealth of Brazil to her cities. Then, in 1609, a group of merchants in Amsterdam engaged Henry Hudson, an Englishman who already had made one passage to America, to find a northeastern route to Asia, around the top of Norway. As captain of the ship *Half Moon*, he left the Netherlands in May. After a month of sailing along the Russian coast of the Arctic Ocean in fog and cold, his crew began to fear a winter of storms and ice. They demanded that Hudson return to warmer latitudes, and to prevent open fighting, he gave orders to turn about.

Hudson did not dare return to Amsterdam yet, for less than six weeks had passed since they had left. So, as he had some letters and maps of Virginia from John Smith, Hudson started across the Atlantic Ocean to see if he could find a north*west* passage to Asia instead.

"Henry Hudson"

For a month or more the *Half Moon* struggled against storms as bad as those off the Russian coast. For six weeks the ship lay off the Grand Banks while the crew repaired storm damage. In August, the *Half Moon* continued her voyage and sailed down the coast as far as the Virginia capes before turning around and heading north again. On August 28, Henry Hudson sailed the *Half Moon* into a broad stream. His secretary, Robert Juet, wrote in his journal that the river was "one of the finest, best and pleasantest rivers in the world." He said that they saw "great white birds, cat-headed and with owl-like bodies." He also described rattlesnakes "with heads like those of dogs and bodies thick as Dutch beer-barrels" which hung head down from the forest trees. No one knows what Juet meant, but this imaginative impression was the first written description of what is now the state of Delaware.

Hudson spent the first day carefully sounding the waters of the bay. Although the *Half Moon* was light of draft, it struck hidden sands. Juet wrote: "Hee that will thoroughly discover this great Bay muste have a small Pinnasse that must draw but four or five foote water, to sound before him."

After seven hours of exploring, Hudson knew from the swiftness of the current and the sandbars that he had found a river rather than a strait. This was not the fabled Northwest Passage. However, he was the first man to explore what he called the South River (to distinguish it from the North River, which later would bear the name Hudson), and his visit to the Delaware River and Bay gave the Dutch a valid claim to that territory for colonization five years later.

Holland Shows Her Strength

When the *Half Moon* returned to Amsterdam, its crew was put aboard another ship and sent back to America—not to explore this time, but to trade with the Indians along the North River for furs. When the ship arrived at the tip of the island which the Indians called Mana-hatta, they built a few rude huts for shelter and thus established the first Dutch trading post in America. They continued to call the island Man-hattan but named the surrounding country New Netherlands.

14

The Dutch were not interested in planting colonies in New Netherlands but only in trading with the Indians for furs. This trade soon proved highly lucrative—so much so that many other merchants in Amsterdam set about getting charters, maps, and information, and hastened to establish trading posts in New Netherlands. The colony thrived.

In 1613 Captain Henry Christiansen and Captain Adriaen Block arrived on the *Fortune* and *Tiger*. Captain Christiansen had brought with him a few goats and rabbits and was prepared to stay all winter on Manhattan. He built four new cabins and assumed the title of governor of New Netherlands.

In November, after Captain Block had left for Holland, an English ship of war sailed into the little harbor at Manhattan under the command of Captain Samuel Argall, later deputy governor of Virginia. Captain Argall had been part of a squadron on its way to Bermuda on a trading trip. When the squadron was caught in a fog, Captain Argall's ship became separated from the others and was blown north by a storm as far as Cape Cod. Argall loaded his ship with fish and set sail for Virginia. Seeking shelter from another storm, he sailed into the bay where the little Dutch settlement of New Netherlands had been made.

Captain Argall was surprised to see the buildings of the trading post in the wilderness. His first reaction was that it must be an outpost of the colony of Virginia. When he learned that it was a Dutch trading post, he demanded that Governor Christiansen surrender to the English. The governor had no choice. He had no way of defending himself against a ship of war.

Captain Argall continued with his load of fish, and as he came to the great bay of the South River, he sailed into it. He named the northern cape of the river's mouth De La Warr, in honor of Sir Thomas West, third Baron De La Warr, the first governor of Virginia. The name "Delawarr" was soon applied to the river and the bay—and many years later to the state that would be formed on the west bank of the river. The spelling was soon changed to Delaware to make it comparable to the English way of pronouncing it.

Explorers Ransomed

Governor Christiansen did not allow his being conquered by the English to affect his original plans, and when Captain Block returned in the spring of 1614, a sturdy, well-built ship, the first to be constructed on Manhattan Island, was waiting for him. It was named the *Unrest*.

The government of Holland had promised to give exclusive trading rights to the company that first submitted an accurate map of the new colony. Captain Block took the *Unrest* and set out to explore what is now Long Island Sound. Captain Cornelius Mey of Hoorn, Holland, took the ship *Fortune* and started south down the New Jersey coast. Not knowing that Argall had already named the north cape De La Warr, Mey called it by his own name. The cape still preserves the name, although the spelling has been changed, and so does the town of Cape May, New Jersey.

To the cape immediately southwest from Cape May (near modern Lewes), he gave his first name, Cornelius, and farther south he named a false cape (now Fenwick's Island) Hinlopen, after a village in Holland. However, many of the colonists preferred to call this southwest cape Cape Hinlopen, and this name became so well attached that, since 1800, all maps place the name Cape Hinlopen (or Henlopen) at this point of land. Many old records state that the southern boundary of Delaware begins at Cape Henlopen, which was true at the time they were written.

When Captain Mey returned to Manhattan, Cornelius Hendricksen took the little yacht *Unrest* and went south again in 1615. He sailed into the great bay and up the South River, where he drew charts, took soundings, and traded with the Indians for otter, mink, and bear skins. He hunted in the great oak forests and said in his report that he "discovered and explored certain lands, a bay and three rivers, situated between 38 and 40 degrees."

At the spot where Wilmington, Delaware, now stands, Hendricksen went ashore to meet with the Indians. Here he was very much surprised to be greeted in his native language by three men who were thought to be dead. They had been sent by the governor of New Netherlands

16

from Fort Nassau (near present-day Albany, New York) on an exploring expedition into the interior. They had followed the Mohawk River and Schoharie Creek, then wandered through a fertile region to the headwaters of the Delaware River. These Dutchmen were the first Europeans to see the lands that would become Pennsylvania.

When they reached the Schuylkill River, where Philadelphia now is, they were captured by the Minquas, or Susquehannock, Indians, who were related to and spoke the same language as the Iroquois. Captain Hendricksen paid the Indians a ransom for the men, and from their stories he wrote a glowing report of the resources of the country lying on either side of the South River. Back in Holland, he immediately asked the States General, the Dutch legislative assembly, to grant him the trading rights between the 38th and 40th degrees of latitude, which included the peninsula between the two bays. The States General, knowing that the colony of Virginia extended north to the 38th degree of latitude and that the colony of Jamestown was only about fifty miles south of that, was afraid they might get into trouble with England, so they refused Captain Hendricksen's request.

Also, Holland had signed a treaty with Spain in 1609, agreeing that she would not trade with the Indies or America until the end of 1621. Although her representatives at Manhattan had not been challenged except by Argall in the year 1613, she could be accused of breaking the treaty if she expanded her colony in America.

As soon as the twelve years' truce expired at the end of 1621, the Dutch West India Company was given a charter by the government of Holland to trade with America. Interest in New Netherlands was immediate. Captain Cornelius Mey was appointed governor of the Dutch colony at New Amsterdam. He brought with him about thirty colonists, Belgian Protestants who had fled to Holland from Catholic persecution. He built new Dutch forts and homes for the colonists. Governor Mey wanted to establish the Dutch claim on the South River, so in 1623 he sent three or four families to make a settlement at what is now Lewes, Delaware. Their names have not been preserved, but they were the first white settlers to live in Delaware.

The treatment of these first few colonists on Delaware soil set the pattern for the future history of the state. The South River was of secondary importance to the Hudson River in the eyes of the Dutch. The river itself was treacherous, with strong currents and many sandy shoals that made navigation dangerous. The fur trade with the Indians was not so profitable as that on the northern river. The only reason for placing settlers on the Delaware River was to keep it recognized as a part of the Dutch claim to the New World.

Therefore, the Dutch governors in New Netherlands did little to help or encourage the colonists on the Delaware River. The settlers were expected to take care of themselves—build their own houses, clear their own land, raise their own food, and protect themselves from the Indians. The first settlement had no governor of its own, being directly under the governors of New Netherlands, who visited it perhaps once or twice but had little communication with it in between.

The settlers built a brick house at Lewes, but the troops sent with them for protection were ordered to go upstream to build their fort some ninety miles away. This fort was named Nassau, just like the one up the Hudson River. It was built on the east bank of the Delaware River opposite where Philadelphia is now. Governor Mey evidently hoped to start a colony far up the river as a trading post, but the fort was too far away from the little group of settlers at Lewes. They were afraid and homesick and soon asked to go back to New Amsterdam. Fort Nassau was abandoned, and the Dutch colony in what is now Delaware was a failure.

The Valley of Swans

All over Europe in the sevententh century, Protestants and Catholics fought for political and religious supremacy. Gustavus II (Gustavus Adolphus), king of Sweden, was one of the great military leaders of the Protestant cause. Gustavus dreamed of a colony for persecuted Protestants in the New World along the Delaware River. In 1626 he granted a charter to the Swedish South Company for exclusive trade with America and stressed in it that such a colony should be founded.

But the war with Poland and the Thirty Years' War following it

18

put an end to Gustavus' dream, and for eight years after the first Dutch attempt at a colony, the land on the Delaware River remained the province of the Leni-Lenape and the great flocks of migrating water birds.

New Netherlands on the Hudson River had continued to grow, having more than two hundred people. In 1629 the West India Company adopted a charter of freedoms and exemptions. To anyone who would settle land within New Netherlands, this charter gave great power, as much as that of a feudal lord. Five such enterprising settlers, called patroons, purchased from the Indians all the land from Cape Henlopen to Bombay Hook—from what is now the southern boundary of Delaware to a point thirty-two miles northward. This was the first purchase in what is now Delaware, and it was registered at Fort Amsterdam by the governor of New Netherlands, Peter Minuit, July 15, 1630.

As their first venture the patroons made a partnership agreement with an experienced navigator, David Pietersen De Vries, of Hoorn, Hol-

David Pietersen De Vries was a native of Hoorn, Holland. As an experienced navigator, he was assigned to command a whaling colony the Dutch wanted to settle on the South River (Delaware River). The settlers landed at what is now Lewes on Delaware Bay and named their colony Zwaanendael because of the many swans there. Today his statue stands atop the front gable of Zwaanendael House in Lewes.

land, authorizing him to establish a whaling colony. De Vries could not come with the first colonists, but sent his ship, the *Walvis*, under the command of Captain Peter Heyes. Heyes brought twenty-eight men, whaling gear, cattle, supplies and a large mastiff dog and landed near the site of present-day Lewes on Lewes Creek in the spring of 1631. Lime, brick, and tiles made up the ballast for the ship and were unloaded to be used as building materials for a large combination dwelling and storehouse within a stockade.

When the *Walvis* sailed into the Delaware River, thousands of geese, ducks, and swans filled the marshes in their semiannual migration. The Dutch settlers named their site Zwaanendael, the Valley of Swans.

Giles Hossett was sent from New Amsterdam on the Hudson River to be in charge of the colony, and after the fields had been prepared and planted, Captain Heyes returned to Holland in the *Walvis*. The twenty-eight Dutchmen worked hard clearing land and planting crops, and Zwaanendael got off to a good start. Hossett made friends with the Indians and even paid them a second time for the land on which the settlement was made. The Indians brought sturgeon, venison, and turkeys to the colonists, and in return the Dutch gave them beer, which they brewed from the maize and persimmons. Six-inch oysters, all kinds of fish, and birds by the thousands helped to make life pleasant.

Misunderstanding and Massacre

However, the loyal Dutchmen could not make the Indians understand the meaning of sovereignty. Hossett painted a coat of arms of the High and Mighty Lords, States General of the Free United Netherlands, on a piece of tin and placed it on a pillar to signify the ownership of the land. He held a ceremony with a salute of guns and a feast of fish, cheese, ham, and fowls with cabbage, boiled fruit puddings, and Dutch beer. The Indians enjoyed the feast but did not understand the meaning of the symbol. One of the chiefs liked the shiny, painted piece of tin and wanted it to make pipes. Unnoticed, he pried the coat of arms off the pillar and took it home.

Like the Lost Colony of North Carolina, no one knows exactly what happened next, but De Vries himself wrote an account of his arrival at Lewes on December 5, 1632. He said that he saw no sign of the settlers as his ship sailed up the river. Ordering his men to battle stations in case of an attack from the Indians, they sailed up the river to the location of Zwaanendael. Every dwelling house and the storehouse had been burned to the ground. The stockade was destroyed. There was no sign of life except the Indians going about their daily tasks.

When De Vries and a few men went ashore, they found skulls and bones of the murdered Dutchmen strewn over the ground. The next day De Vries coaxed an Indian to come aboard the ship. From him the captain began to learn the gruesome details of the massacre. After questioning many other Indians, he pieced together the following story.

When the Indian chief took the tin coat of arms, Hossett and the settlers were angry at the desecration of what they considered an almost holy symbol. Some of the Indians said that in order to please the Dutch, they killed the chief who had committed the crime and took his head to Hossett, which made him even angrier, and he then killed some of the Indians. Others said that Hossett killed the chief himself. Whichever way it happened, the Indians decided to take revenge on the white people.

When all the colonists, except the officer in charge of the store and one of the men who was sick, had gone to work in the fields, three of the boldest Indians approached the store with a load of beaver skins. They began to bargain with the officer, and he went into an upstairs room where the trade items were kept. As he came down the ladder, the Indians split his head in two with an ax and left him dead on the floor. Next they killed the sick man. The huge mastiff dog which the colonists had brought with them was chained in the yard. The Indians had always been afraid of the dog, never having seen one so large or fierce. They shot at least twenty-five arrows into the animal before he finally died.

When they left the stockade, the three leaders were joined by a group of braves, and together they went to the field where the thirty Dutchmen were working. The Indians had always been friendly, and the farmers did not suspect any danger. With a surprise attack the Indians killed every one of the white men. Then they butchered the Dutch cattle and held a triumphal feast.

21

De Vries sailed back to Holland in the summer of 1633, and no attempt was made to send more Dutch colonists to Zwaanendael. Although the Dutch colony at New Amsterdam continued to flourish and Dutch ships occasionally sailed up the Delaware River to the site of abandoned Fort Nassau to trade for furs with the Indians, another five years passed with only the Indians and the migrating birds living along the shore of the great Delaware River.

The Beginning of Border Problems

Although it was destroyed, the Zwaanendael settlement had a permanent effect on the history of the land on the west bank of the Delaware River. England claimed all the territory from North Carolina to Maine, but Holland had been able to make a strong settlement at New Amsterdam on the Hudson River. When in 1632 Cecilius Calvert, the second Lord Baltimore in the Kingdom of Ireland, obtained a tract of land for a colony, the charter limited the lands granted with the Latin words *hactenus inculta,* or "previously uncultivated." The colony of Zwaanendael had been "cultivated," and therefore the area on the west shore of the Delaware River could be said to be excluded from the Maryland grant. For nearly two hundred years, *hactenus inculta* and Zwaanendael played an important part in the history of Delaware.

The Zwaanendael House at Lewes, erected in 1931, is a small-scale adaption of the ancient Town Hall at Hoorn, Holland, birthplace of Captain David Pietersen De Vries, who organized the first Dutch colony sent to the Delaware River in 1631. The statue on top of the gable is of De Vries.

CHAPTER THREE

The Dream of a Swedish King

In 1630, King Gustavus Adolphus invaded Germany and conquered a tract of land extending from the borders of Hungary to the banks of the Rhine River and from the Lake of Constance to the Baltic Sea.

Gustavus Adolphus appointed himself the protector of the Lutheran Protestants who were being driven out of several Catholic countries and regions, and he began to think of the New World as a place where all Protestants could settle and live according to their consciences. Having talked with William Usselinx, a Dutch explorer who had been there, he dreamed of this Protestant colony on the banks of the Delaware River. Gustavus talked about his plan with many of his advisers, but he was killed in the battle at Lützen in 1632, and his only child, a little six-year-old daughter named Christina, succeeded him as queen of Sweden. During her minority the kingdom was governed by the five highest officers of state, the principal one being Chancellor Axel Oxenstjerna. Oxenstjerna had studied for the ministry when he was a young man and was as interested in promoting the Protestant cause as his king had been.

Three Angry Dutchmen

William Usselinx of Antwerp became disenchanted with the Dutch West India Company because it was interested only in short-term profits from trading with the Indians. Usselinx wanted to colonize for a long-term investment. He resigned as one of the directors of the West India Company, and after Gustavus' death he approached Chancellor Oxenstjerna about settling a colony on the Delaware River. Oxenstjerna agreed to subsidize the New Sweden Company, and Usselinx looked around for some partners. He found that he was not the only one dissatisfied with the Dutch West India Company.

Peter Minuit, who had bought Manhattan Island from the Indians, was angry also because some of his enemies charged that he had stolen Dutch West India Company funds. Minuit called himself the "Midnight Man" and flew from the masthead of his ship a flag with a black bat as his personal totem. He was eager to break up the monopoly the Dutch West India Company had on American trade and gladly chipped in one eighth of the twenty-four thousand guilder capital stock of the New Sweden Company.

Samuel Blommaert, who had been one of the five patroons from New Netherlands to put up the money for Zwaanendael, was angry at the Dutch West India Company because he felt that it had not paid him enough for his losses from the massacre of that colony. He took the cash they did pay him and invested it in the New Sweden Company.

Each of these three angry Dutchmen was well acquainted with the financial process of founding a colony as well as with the New World itself. Usselinx was the promoter, Blommaert the administrator, and Minuit the coordinator.

Chancellor Axel Oxenstjerna drew up the charter for the New Sweden Company. Ignoring the Dutch and English claims, it stated that the company was organized to colonize the entire coast of North America from Florida to Newfoundland. Backed by the full support of Sweden, the three Dutchmen set about gathering settlers and supplies for New Sweden on the Delaware.

In spite of her great military strength, Sweden was having a problem with her next-door neighbors, the Finns. No matter how she tried to control them, these men from the great forest crossed the border and helped themselves to land, burning the trees and killing off the wild game wherever it suited their fancy. The Swedes feared the Finns because they were thought to practice witchcraft and to bring disease and disaster by means of black magic. New Sweden would be a good place for the unwelcome Finns. They were rounded up for deportation.

The "Midnight Man" Founds New Sweden

Other undesirables were also thought to be good settlers: a man who shot moose, married men found guilty of adultery, soldiers who had deserted from the army, a man who had cut down cherry trees in an orchard. These people were not hardened criminals but misfits who did not conform to the rigid laws of the country. Most of them were hard working and adjusted well to the primitive conditions of the new colony.

Peter Minuit was appointed director of the first expedition, and preparations were kept secret from Holland until just before the sailing date. By December 1637 two ships, the *Kalmar Nyckel* (*Key of Kalmar*) and a smaller vessel named *Grip,* were ready.

The two small ships butted their way slowly through the stormy Atlantic. Besides supplies and a heavy load of axes, mirrors, toys, and cheap brass chains to trade with the Indians, the ships also carried a cargo of wines to be sold in the West Indies. Food ran short, and many of the passengers and crew were sick. The fear that a spark might ignite the ton and a half of powder stored in the hold was always present. Minuit's black bat flying from the masthead seemed to be a sign of certain doom.

Early in March of 1638 the ships arrived at Jamestown, Virginia. Jerome Hawley, secretary of the Virginia colony, was upset by the appearance of the Swedes and wrote to the secretary of the London Company:

> The ship remained here about ten days, to refresh with wood and water, during which time the master of said ship made known that both himself and another ship of his company were bound for Delaware Bay, which is the confines of Virginia and New England, and there they pretend to make a plantation and to plant tobacco, which the Dutch do so already in Hudson's River. . . .

Ignoring the concern of the secretary of Virginia, Minuit and his two shiploads of Swedes continued their journey to the Delaware

Heading up the first settlement of New Sweden, Peter Minuit sailed the *Kalmar Nyckel* into Delaware Bay. They first stopped near the site of the old Dutch colony, Zwaanendael (Lewes), then on up the river to The Rocks, near present-day Wilmington. Here they unloaded and built Fort Christina. Minuit's black-bat flag is not visible in this picture.

River. Just as the shad and sturgeon began running up the rivers to spawn and the marshes were covered with the migrating waterfowl, the two Swedish ships sailed into Delaware Bay. The banks on both sides of the river were filled with the lodges of the Minquas Indians, who had come from their homes farther northwest up the river to catch fish and hunt fowl.

Minuit did not want to make his settlement where the Indians had their hunting grounds even though De Vries had made friends with the Indians after the massacre of Zwaanendael. He sailed on up the river to the point of rocks where Captain Hendricksen had met the three captive Dutchmen twenty-three years earlier. Near the place where

27

the two Indian boys watched the Canada geese each year, a little stream ran into the Fishing (Brandywine) River. Minuit named it Christina Creek in honor of the then twelve-year-old queen of Sweden. Here, on the solid shelf of rocks at the confluence of creek and river, the settlers and soldiers unloaded the boats and established their colony of New Sweden. The Rocks, as it is called, is now within the city limits of Wilmington.

On March 29 Minuit once again bought the land from the Indians. The deed was signed on board the *Kalmar Nyckel* by five Indian chiefs

This monument marks the spot called The Rocks, where Peter Minuit landed with the first Swedish settlers and built Fort Christina.

When the Swedes landed at The Rocks, near what is now Wilmington, they were greeted by friendly Indians of the Leni-Lenape people. Peter Minuit, who was in command of the expedition, immediately bought the land from the Indian chiefs, and the deed was signed on board the *Kalmar Nyckel.*

and by Minuit and his officers. The soldiers went to work building a fort, which they also named Christina, and Minuit sent the *Grip* on a trading expedition while he bought furs from the Indians to take back to Sweden.

It took less than a month for Governor William Kieft in New Amsterdam on the Hudson River to hear of the Swedes' arrival on the Delaware River. He promptly wrote a letter of protest to Peter Minuit, saying:

> I William Kieft, Director-General of New Netherlands, residing on the Island of Manhattan, in New Amsterdam . . . make known to the Hon. Peter Minuit, who calls himself commissioner in the service of her royal majesty of Sweden, that the whole South River, in New Netherlands, has been in our possession many years. . . . If you proceed with the building of forts, and cultivating the lands, and trading in furs, or engage further in any thing to our prejudice, [we] will not be answerable for any mishaps, effusion of blood, troubles and disasters which your company might suffer in future. . . . This done Thursday, being the 6th of May, anno, 1638.

Unique Homes—Log Cabins

As soon as the colonists had landed, Peter Minuit raised his black-bat flag and assigned each man to his task. While the soldiers built a fort, the Finns and Swedish farmers began to clear land for houses and fields. The work of clearing suited the Finns fine. They were strong men and swung their axes with joy, cutting down the tall virgin trees and stripping the branches cleanly from the trunks. They were about to introduce to the New World a structure that was to have a profound effect on American life and history. This structure was the log cabin.

Men brought to America the modes of building to which they were accustomed back home. The English, Dutch, and French, who had settled other parts of the continent, came from lands where trees and lumber were relatively scarce and had to be used sparingly. At home and in America they built frame houses sided with shingle, wattle-and-daub (a primitive stucco), or brick—dwelling places whose construction required skilled labor and much time. But Finland and Sweden—like Germany and Russia, whose peasants also commonly built log houses— were thickly forested. Where wood was plentiful, house walls could be erected of full-sized logs, and a small team of semiskilled men might "roll up" a snug family home in a single day. Now in New Sweden, where wood was as easy to find as at home, they set to work.

The workmen were chiefly Finns. They cut cedar tres of equal size and length, and after trimming off the branches, they notched each log near the ends—a saddle notch, it was called. An experienced cabin builder always made sure that the side of the log that was to face outward was notched deeper than the inner face, so that rainwater would drip toward the outside. After laying the first two logs parallel on the site selected for a house, the workmen then placed the next two logs at right angles to the first two, with the notches fitting carefully into one an-

As soon as the colonists had landed, Peter Minuit assigned the soldiers to build a fort, while the farmers began to clear land for houses and fields.

By 1641 the colony of New Sweden had settled down to a self-reliant community with families as well as soldiers and workers. Although a Swede (left) usually felt himself above the Finnish peasant (right), the Finns proved themselves most useful in cutting down the trees and building the first log cabins in America.

other. Two more logs were placed in the same direction as the first and so on until four walls were as high as desired—usually one room and a loft was high enough. Shorter logs formed the gable at either end, held together by lengthwise logs of small dimension. These roofbeams were then finished with thatch, bark, or shingles.

When he had completed his log cabin, the Finn cut a doorway into it, in which he hung a door of slab on leather hinges. These doorways were cut low to conserve heat, and because most of the Swedes and Finns were tall, they had to duck as they entered. Small windows were usually cut, too, and covered with oiled paper. In one corner—a position typical of Scandinavian construction—there was a huge fireplace, plastered inside with clay, with a wooden chimney, which served for cooking and heated the house in cold weather. Thus, because of the thick, solid log walls and the snug fit of the notched corners, the log-cabin dweller had a home that was warm in winter and cool in summer.

Later, when more time for building—or more skilled craftsmanship —was available, the settlers of New Sweden sometimes refined this technique. Instead of using round logs, they "hewed" them—that is, squared them to the shape of a beam—so that they could be fitted together without gaps. The ends of these hewn logs were cut into dovetails or lap joints, so that they meshed snugly at the corners without overlap, like the back of a well-made drawer. Some of these more carefully built structures—a hewn-log cabin was usually called a log house— were planked inside, and when a shipment of glass arrived in New Sweden, many had true windows in them.

But in early days, the cruder cabin was good enough for the newcomers. Their beds were made of piles of grass or dry leaves laid on a dirt floor or a plank "bedstead" fastened by cleats into the walls of the cabin. Slabs of puncheon—a log cut in two with the flat side up— made tables, stools, shelves. If there was a sleeping loft above, wooden pegs were driven into the wall in a vertical line, to form a crude ladder.

The Swedes and Finns did not popularize the log cabin—that was done chiefly by the Germans in Pennsylvania at a later period—but they were the first to build it on this side of the Atlantic. English and Dutch settlers, recognizing the practical virtues of such a versatile building technique, eventually adopted it. Later as German and Scotch-Irish settlers moved west, they took this kind of house with them, and in time the log cabin became the symbol of the frontier—the cutting edge of civilization moving relentlessly across the land.

Introduction of the Sauna

As soon as they had finished their own homes, the Swedes and Finns built their *bastu*. These one-room buildings were located near the riverbank and were used for steam bathing, as are our present-day saunas. The *bastu* was carefully chinked between the logs to make it tight, and a big fireplace was built into one end of the room. Inside,

33

two wide shelves were placed, one above the other along the wall opposite the fireplace.

At bath time a roaring fire was made, and rocks were pushed into it to heat. When the rocks were hot, water was poured over them to make steam. The Swedes and Finns first lay naked on the upper shelf, where the steam was hottest. Then they moved down to the lower shelf and whipped their bodies lightly with bundles of birch branches to cause the blood to circulate faster. After an hour in the steam bath, the hardy bathers ran naked from the *bastu* and dived into the cold river water to close the pores of their bodies. In the winter, they rolled in the snow.

The Swedes worked hard and played hard, and in order to maintain their energy they ate four hearty meals a day. At each meal they had either domestic or wild meat. With it they ate beans, peas, and turnip greens served always with large loaves of rye bread with fresh sweet butter and honey.

They washed down the food with swigs of rum punch made of water, sugar, lemon juice, and spirits. On cold winter nights the rum punch was heated by plunging a red-hot poker into the bowl.

The Swedes made syllibub by squirting milk directly from the cow's teats into a bowl of wine made from the wild grapes, causing it to foam. Another drink made with rum, eggs, milk, and allspice was first introduced by these settlers. It is now known as eggnog.

Although Holland claimed the land on both sides of the Delaware River, Governor Kieft knew that he was not strong enough to oppose the Swedish colony. He continued to protest against the intrusion, but Minuit laughed at him and disregarded his threats.

Minuit, when he was governor of New Netherlands, had removed the soldiers and abandoned Fort Nassau on the Delaware River. Governor Kieft decided that, in order to protect the Dutch interests there, he should garrison it again. The ship he sent with troops to station at Fort Nassau stopped at Christina and demanded that Minuit and his Swedish colonists leave. Minuit defied the Dutch to put him out and threatened to blow the ship out of the river. The Dutch captain saw that the guns of Fort Christina were trained on his ship, and he left, muttering threats.

Peter Minuit now prepared to return home. In three months he had bought land from the Indians, built Fort Christina, helped his colonists get settled, and scared off the Dutch. He sailed from New Sweden in June in the *Kalmar Nyckel* for the island of St. Christopher in the West Indies to trade the cargo of wine he had brought with him. While there, he went aboard a Dutch ship one evening to visit with the captain. A storm came up, and the ship was blown out of the harbor. Neither the ship nor anyone aboard was ever seen again. The crew of the *Kalmar Nyckel* sailed Minuit's ship back to Sweden.

CHAPTER FOUR

The Dutch Governor's Goal

The Swedish government bought the shares of the Dutch investors who had worked so hard to start New Sweden, and in 1640 a second expedition was sent out from Sweden in charge of Peter Hollender Ridder. Governor Ridder brought with him more colonists and a Lutheran clergyman, Reorus Torkillus, the first Lutheran minister to serve in America. In the fall of that year fifty Dutch settlers arrived under Swedish protection. About a year later the *Kalmar Nyckel* returned with fifty Swedish soldiers, Finns with wives and children, farm laborers, a bookkeeper, a tailor, a millwright, and a blacksmith. They brought with them goats, horses, sheep, cattle, grain, farm and cooking implements, building materials, and trinkets to trade with the Indians.

Governor Ridder was glad to see the new settlers and soldiers. In the year and a half that he had been governor, he had been threatened by both the English and the Dutch. A group of English settlers who lived in Connecticut became discontented and decided that the Delaware River would be a better place to live. They decided on Salem Creek on the east side of the river as a site for their settlement, and since the English were on the far side of the river, Ridder thought that they would bother the Dutch at Fort Nassau more than they would the Swedes. As he suspected, the Dutch promptly sent an expedition down from Fort Nassau and ordered them to get out. The frightened English packed up and moved, but only across the river to the Swedish side. They bought land from the Indians at the mouth of the Schuylkill and settled there.

Big Belly

Governor Ridder wrote a report of this new settlement to the authorities in Sweden and sent it on the returning *Kalmar Nyckel*. He asked for more soldiers and colonists to reinforce New Sweden.

On January 3, 1643, three Swedish ships of war, the *Swan* and *Charitas* and an armed transport called the *Fame*, arrived at Lewes in the midst of a snowstorm. The *Fame* lost three anchors, her mainmast, and some of her sails. Finally, six weeks later, they reached Christina.

On board the flagship was a new Swedish governor, Johan Björnsson Printz, a four-hundred-pound cavalry major of the Swedish Army. The Indians took one look at the giant and dubbed him Big Belly.

Governor Printz brought his own horses with him, and every available space of the ships was filled with household equipment and cloth-

Four-hundred-pound Major Johan Printz was promptly dubbed Big Belly by the Indians when he arrived to take over the governorship of New Sweden. In spite of his enormous size, Printz displayed much energy in stocking the colony and building forts along the river.

ing. Stopping at the West Indies, he had filled all remaining crevices with oranges and lemons. After he looked over the struggling colony, he immediately ordered from New Amsterdam enough livestock to double the number in the colony. He also bought feed for the horses and cattle to carry them through the winter and food for the settlers.

The arrival of Printz with the largest fleet ever to enter the Delaware River was proof to the Dutch that Sweden was serious about making a permanent settlement in America. Printz brought with him a set of formal instructions containing twenty-eight articles. He was to encourage sincere piety toward Almighty God and to maintain the Lutheran religion. He was to see that the children of the colony were well educated. He was to promote any industry by which he could make a profit: furs, cattle, sheep, grain, tobacco. He was to plant mulberry trees to feed silkworms from which to make silk. And he was to try to find some way to make salt from seawater. He was instructed to be friendly with the Dutch and English as well as with the Indians.

Before he left to return to Sweden, Governor Ridder explained to Governor Printz that he had bought from the Indians all the land on both sides of the Delaware River as far up as the falls—now Trenton, New Jersey. Ridder suggested that Printz build a fort on the New Jersey side below the mouth of the Varkens Kill, directly opposite the English settlement at the mouth of the Schuylkill River, to control the traffic of the river.

A Palace in the Wilderness

Since Ridder's purchase extended well past the location of present-day Philadelphia, Printz chose Tinicum Island, about three Swedish miles above Fort Christina, for his palace and the capital of the colony. Within eight months Printz's soldiers had completed two new forts of great hemlock logs. As Governor Ridder had suggested, he built one at Varken's Kill and named it Fort Elfsborg. It was equipped with eight guns to halt any ship that might come up the river headed for Fort Nassau.

In October of 1643, David Pietersen De Vries, founder of the ill-fated Dutch colony at Zwaanendael twelve years earlier, sailed up the river toward Fort Nassau. At Fort Elfsborg his ship was fired on, and he was ordered to strike his flag. After he had done so, he was forced to row to the fort in a small boat to obtain Printz's consent to sail higher up the river.

Governor Printz next invited Captain George Lamberton, a leader of the Connecticut group, to visit him. The Englishman put on his best clothes, expecting a banquet, but Printz clapped him into chains. He accused Lamberton of inciting the Indians to rebellion and trading illegally and ordered him to be tried. A Swedish court convicted Lamberton and ordered him to pay a fine of beaver skins and to take his Connecticut settlers and leave the river.

Having driven the English out, Printz took over the English site and on it built another fort. To guard the Indian trail, where Little Cobb's Creek flows into Darby Creek, just south of modern Darby, Pennsylvania, he built a fort which he named Vasa, and about a quarter of a mile beyond it the governor built the first gristmill on the Delaware River.

Feeling that the river was properly fortified, Governor Printz turned his attention to building a suitable palace for himself and his family. He selected a high site with a view of the surrounding land and river. Using the soldiers for labor, he built a hewn-log mansion, which he called Printz Hall, with real glass windows brought from Sweden. The palace had a library with books said to be worth $200, and Madame Printz's jewelry was valued at $1,200. Account books showed that the governor and his wife had clothes costing more than $2,000. Those were large sums in those days.

Besides being an elegant home, the mansion also acted as a storehouse in case of a siege. It contained three thousand pounds of salt pork and a quarter of a ton of salted beef, eighty pounds of cheese, and a hundred pounds of candles. A good quantity of rum and spirits was also kept on hand at all times.

Governor Printz did not enjoy his palace long. On a cold November night in 1645 the sentry built a fire to keep himself warm. It got out of control, set the wooden mansion on fire, and burned it to the ground. Although Governor Printz promptly began to rebuild his palace, he was forced to spend the winter with the common people at Christina.

Meanwhile, Printz constantly reminded the Swedish government that he needed more soldiers, farmers, and supplies. Among the "supplies" he mentioned were women. A number of Swedish families had come together to Christina, but there were few single women of marriageable age, and the single men were not content without wives. The company ignored his request to send women, but some of the women in Sweden began to hear rumors that the men in New Sweden were making a profit and getting rich. In July 1649, the *Katt* left Sweden with military supplies, seventy Finns, and a number of young ladies who had volunteered to go to the colony to become wives of the single men.

The passengers on the *Katt* came to a tragic end, however. The ship

Peter Stuyvesant was the aggressive governor of New Amsterdam when Johan Printz was sent to govern the little colony of Swedes on the Delaware River. Believing the Swedes were a threat to his colony, he sailed a fleet up the South River past the Swedish forts and erected a fort at what is now New Castle. Eventually, in 1655 he gained the surrender of the entire colony.

was caught in a hurricane off Puerto Rico and was blown off course. The men and women aboard were captured by a pirate ship and sold for slaves.

Although Governor Printz tried to build up the colony of New Sweden, he grew more and more unjust in his administration. He treated the people as his slaves, forcing them to work without pay as servants at Printz Hall and on his plantation. A great number of the colonists protested. They signed a petition listing their grievances and presented it to the governor, begging him to change his ways. Printz was furious. He arrested the leader, tried him for treason, and had him instantly executed. He proclaimed the other signers rebels and published a formal denial of their complaints.

The Impertinent Dutch Governor

Governor Printz built New Sweden to its greatest power. His Swedish forts controlled the Delaware River for ten years, and he had forced the colonists to build mills, houses, boats, wharves, and trading posts.

Meanwhile, Peter Stuyvesant came to New Netherlands as the governor. He had under his rule a well-established colony at New Amsterdam as well as men, money, and ships. He was not afraid of Governor Printz, knowing that he had neither the manpower nor the support from Sweden that Stuyvesant had from Holland.

Before Printz knew what was going on, Stuyvesant sailed a fleet of ships, with drums and cannon blaring, up the Delaware River without asking Printz's permission or striking his flag. Printz blustered, swore, and threatened to blow the Dutch ships out of the river, but he was powerless to stop Stuyvesant's fleet.

Governor Stuyvesant landed about six miles down the river from Christina. Here, on the present site of New Castle, he built a fort which he named Casimir in honor of Count Ernest Casimir of Nassau, for whom Fort Nassau had been named. He abandoned Fort Nassau and brought the Dutch families and soldiers from there to the new fort. Because Fort Casimir was farther downstream than Fort Christina, the Dutch now controlled the entrance to the river.

Fort Casimir was built on the present site of New Castle by Peter Stuyvesant in defiance of Governor Johan Printz of New Sweden. Three years later, the Swedes seized the fort, which so infuriated Stuyvesant that he built the largest fleet of ships ever seen in America and not only captured Fort Casimir but forced the surrender of the entire Swedish colony.

Printz sent a strong protest to Stuyvesant, but the governor of New Netherlands ignored it. In 1653 Printz sent his son on an English ship to Sweden to ask for enough men and supplies to drive the Dutch from the Delaware. At the end of the year, however, he had heard nothing from Sweden. He left New Sweden in charge of his son-in-law and returned to Sweden. Just as he arrived, a ship was preparing to leave for America. Supplies, more settlers, and a new governor, Johan Classon Rising, set sail on the *Orn* on February 10, 1654.

Johan Rising brought with him an engineer, Per Mårtensson Lindeström, whose *Geography of America* is still one of the best sources of Swedish history in America.

Rising had been given orders in Sweden to get back any of her lands that had been taken by others. He was to use only peaceful means, however, and if he met with resistance, he was to move the entire settlement to another location. In spite of these orders, on Trinity Sunday, May 21, 1654, when he sailed into the Delaware River and anchored before Fort Casimir, he demanded that the Dutch surrender. This was the first time that anyone had opposed the little Dutch fort, and the garrison was taken completely by surprise. It meekly surrendered.

Governor Rising manned the fort with Swedish soldiers and renamed it Fort Trinity. Leaving Captain Swen Schute in charge, he sailed triumphantly up the river to Christina.

Unlike Printz, Governor Rising treated the people fairly, and in response they worked hard. Within a year they had doubled the land under cultivation, cleared overgrown roads, and built new ones. Per Mårtensson Lindeström, the engineer, drew up a plan to expand the village of Christina. The forts along the river were strengthened so that they withstood the winter floods and ice. In little more than a year, New Sweden had again become a thriving community of about three hundred colonists.

Return to Fort Casimir

When Governor Peter Stuyvesant heard that Rising had taken his fort, he promptly set about preparing for revenge. However, he did not want Governor Rising to know his plans, so he worked in secret. For the next year, Rising was allowed to govern in peace.

During that time, Governor Rising held a council with the Leni-Lenape at Printz Hall on Tinicum Island. Ten chiefs came, and Chief Naaman spoke for them. He said that the white people were pushing the Indians back from the river, from which they obtained much of their food.

Rising told the chiefs that the Swedes wished to live peacefully with them. Then he distributed gifts among them. After several days of talks, the Indians agreed to the former boundaries and went away

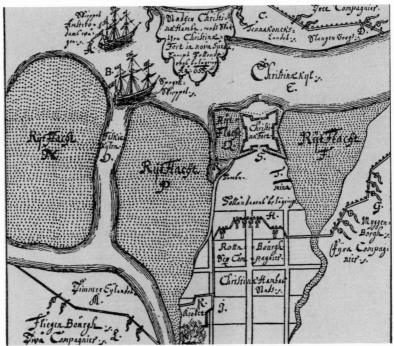

Per Mårtensson Lindeström, a Swedish engineer, came to New Sweden with Governor Johan Classon Rising in 1654. A year after his arrival Lindeström was a witness to the capture of Fort Christina by the Dutch and drew this map of the siege.

quietly. The autumn and winter of 1654 passed without trouble from either the Indians or the Dutch. The Swedish settlers planted their crops as usual and expected a good harvest in the fall of 1655.

Governor Peter Stuyvesant, however, was ready to strike. With a squadron of seven armed ships and transports, carrying more than six hundred men, he set sail from New Amsterdam about the middle of August. The Indians learned what was happening and sent word from one village to another until finally the news reached Christina.

When an Indian messenger informed Governor Rising that the Dutch fleet was headed for Delaware Bay, he hurriedly sent reinforcements to Fort Trinity with supplies and ammunition. He wrote Commander Swen

Schute to defend the fort if it was attacked, but if the Dutch came in peace, to assure them that the Swedes were friendly.

Stuyvesant's fleet arrived at Fort Trinity on August 31. Commander Schute, knowing that his small force could not withstand an attack, waited to see what Stuyvesant would do. Unopposed, Stuyvesant landed a company of men just above the fort and began to build a breastwork. When Commander Schute walked out to the breastwork for a parley with Stuyvesant, the governor ordered him to surrender, and Schute offered no resistance. Aboard the flagship, Schute signed articles of surrender, which stated that the Swedes could march out with their colors and retain their private property. Stuyvesant then announced that the name of the fort was again Fort Casimir.

Conquest Without Bloodshed

Fort Trinity was taken so suddenly and quietly that Governor Rising did not know about it until the next day, when he sent a few men to

Here Dutch Peter Stuyvesant and Swedish Johan Rising clash hand-to-hand at the attack on Fort Christina—an artist's misconception, for history declares that Fort Christina was taken without a fight.

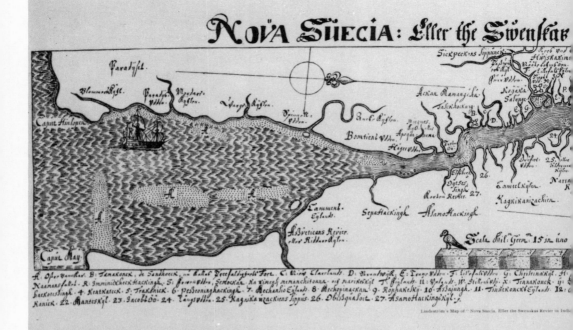

A map taken from *The Swedish Settlements on the Delaware, 1638–1664* by Amandus Johnson. The title translates as "New Sweden or the Swedes River in the West Indies."

reinforce the garrison. When they landed, they were ordered to surrender. In a skirmish the Swedes were captured except for two men who escaped and managed to get back to the boat.

When they reached Fort Christina and told Rising, he thought that the Dutch only wanted the fort, which had originally been built by them. Stuyvesant, however, sent his transport ships up the Brandywine and placed four cannon on Timber Island, pointing toward Fort Christina. After putting cannon at three other places, completely surrounding Fort Christina, he sailed his armed vessels into the mouth of the Brandywine River.

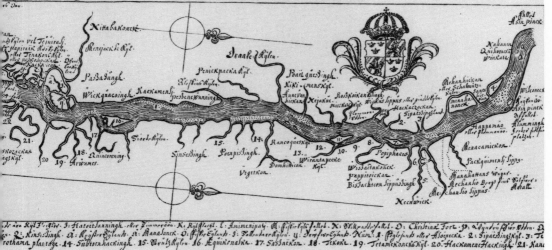

ER, IN INDIA OCCIDENTALI·

(the Swedes' River in the West Indies). From Lindeström's *Geographia.*

The next day, Governor Stuyvesant, in a letter sent by an Indian messenger, ordered Governor Rising either to leave the country or to surrender and live under Dutch rule. Governor Rising called his men into a council of war. They replied to Governor Stuyvesant that, if the Dutch should fire on them, they would defend themselves.

Stuyvesant did not even reply. He ordered his soldiers to round up the Swedes' cattle, goats, swine, and poultry, and kill them, then to burn the houses outside the fort. Rising and his men watched helplessly. In his report to the Swedish government, Rising wrote that they could not resist because they had scarcely a single round of ammunition for their guns.

Rising knew that he could not defend Fort Christina, but he made one last attempt to save it. He wrote a long letter of protest to Stuyvesant, saying that the government of Sweden would hold the government of Holland accountable for what Stuyvesant was doing. Stuyvesant replied that the Delaware River belonged to Holland and that the Swedes had no right to be there in the first place. If they wished to remain, it must be under Dutch rule.

Some of the men had already deserted from Fort Christina, and others were sick and wanted to surrender. On September 13, Stuyvesant and Rising held a conference on the hill behind the fort. One last time, Rising protested. Stuyvesant still demanded the surrender of Fort Christina and the whole river. Rising refused and returned to Fort Christina to order his men to defend it.

The next day Stuyvesant sent a messenger to tell Rising that, if he did not surrender within twenty-four hours, the Dutch would take the fort by force. Rising called another council of the whole garrison. They voted to surrender.

The Dutch did not want to destroy the colony of New Sweden. They simply wanted the Delaware River for their trading ground. The surrender treaty stated that any Swedes who wanted to stay in the colony could do so but that they must take an oath of allegiance to Holland. Those who did not wish to do so could go back to Sweden.

Peter Stuyvesant had achieved his goal. He had proved himself a skillful leader. Waging war with the most powerful fleet and army that had ever been seen in North America, he nevertheless had won an important victory without the loss of a single victim on either side.

New Sweden no longer existed, but most of the Swedes remained at Christina, whose name was changed by the Dutch to Altena. The Swedes went about their daily lives as they had done since the founding of the colony seventeen years before.

CHAPTER FIVE

The Three Lower Counties

G overnor Peter Stuyvesant returned to New Amsterdam, and on November 29, 1655, he appointed Jean Paul Jaquet governor of all the settlements on the Delaware River. Governor Jaquet left New Amsterdam for New Amstel, the little town just outside Fort Casimir. New Amstel was to be the capital of the Dutch-controlled colony, in place of Christina, because it was farther down the Delaware River and could control the entrance to the river better than the upper town.

Jaquet immediately set about establishing Dutch order. He extended the streets behind the fort, laying off lots sixty feet wide by three hundred feet deep. Each lot holder was given as much land outside the village as he agreed to cultivate.

Another of Jaquet's duties was to collect taxes on the exports and imports in and out of the river brought by foreign ships. The *Mercurius* had sailed from Sweden before the news reached that country that the Dutch had captured New Sweden. Because the ship carried Swedes and Finns who had come as colonists, Jaquet refused to let them land. When the Indians near New Amstel heard that the ship was delayed, they quietly rowed out to board it at night.

The next morning they started piloting the *Mercurius* up the river. Jaquet did not dare fire on the Indians for fear of starting an uprising, and the ship went safely past the guns of Fort Casimir. The colonists were landed near Tinicum, where they were welcomed by the Swedish families who lived there.

Meanwhile, the news reached Holland and Sweden that New Sweden had been captured by the Dutch. The Swedish government protested to

The Old Dutch House in New Castle is one of the oldest remaining houses in Delaware. The central chimney served to heat the house in winter and for cooking all year round.

the States General of Holland, but the protest was ignored. The Swedes had their hands full with the war they were waging against Poland and were in no position to go to war with Holland over their little colony in America.

Growth of a Dutch Colony

During the next year the Dutch West India Company recognized both the necessity and the profit in colonizing what had been the Swedish colony. Company officials wrote home begging for more and more settlers. If Holland was to retain possession of the South River and to reap its fruits, the colony must be properly peopled. The West India Company therefore solicited aid from the city of Amsterdam, asking her to help colonize an area on the South River where the soil was richest but the population smallest. The governors of Amsterdam agreed that such colonization might be profitable, and in the summer of 1656 they started planning to send colonists to New Amstel.

The land on the west side of the South River was now divided into two colonies. The upper one, including Fort Christina and the surrounding land, extended down the river to Bombay Hook. This was called the Colony of the Company. The other started at Bombay Hook and extended downriver past New Amstel and was called the Colony of the City, meaning Amsterdam.

Jean Paul Jaquet was replaced on April 20, 1657, by Jacob Alrichs, whose title was vice-director. When he arrived with about two hundred colonists and soldiers with their families and servants, he found only about twenty families, mostly Swedes, living at New Amstel. Soon he began building a town hall of logs, two stories high, as well as a wharf and storehouse, a bakehouse, a guardhouse, a forge, and brick kilns. On April 25, 1658, Evert Pietersen landed at New Amstel. His official title was schoolmaster and comforter of the sick, and he was the first recorded schoolmaster in the colony. He immediately set up a school and by August had twenty-five pupils.

In spite of these improvements, the Dutch colony had many problems. The colonists had planted crops, but heavy rains ruined them and food was scarce. A fever epidemic broke out, during which the surgeon, Alrichs' wife, and several children died.

While the epidemic was still raging, the ship *Mill* arrived from Holland, bringing many new immigrants, among whom were several children from the Orphan House in Amsterdam. The new settlers increased the population of New Amstel to more than six hundred people, but the ship had brought no provisions, and the colony was approaching starvation. Industry was at a standstill while the demand for higher wages increased. Alrichs wrote to Governor Stuyvesant that their only hope for survival was provisions from New Amsterdam.

To add to this misery, agents from Lord Baltimore rode into the southern part of the colony and spent several days stirring up the Indians and threatening the settlers. When they returned to Maryland, the rumor spread that five hundred men from Maryland would march on the colony and take it for the English. The frightened colonists began to pack up and leave. Many of the soldiers of the garrison in the fort deserted and fled to Virginia or Maryland. Governor Alrichs sent a messenger to New Amsterdam to ask Governor Stuyvesant for reinforcements. Stuyvesant sent sixty soldiers overland with four men to act as agents for the company. They arrived in Patuxent, Maryland, a week later, where they met with Governor Josias Fendall and his council. They discussed the boundary dispute, but no conclusion was reached, and the soldiers and agents returned to New Amsterdam.

During these discussions, business in the Dutch colony was suspended, and everyone prepared for flight. Fifty persons moved to Maryland and Virginia, leaving scarcely thirty families at New Amstel, where only ten soldiers remained in the fort. In the midst of these troubles, Alrichs died, leaving the government to Alexander D'Hinoyossa, his lieutenant.

D'Hinoyossa persuaded the burgomasters of Amsterdam to make him director of the colony. He planned to make it his personal empire, but before he could achieve this the English took a hand in the affairs of the Dutch colonies, both at New Amsterdam and at New Amstel.

By this time, England had well-established settlements south of the Delaware River in Virginia and Maryland. North of New Amsterdam the English settlements spread from Connecticut and Long Island to what is now Maine. Holland had made no colonies between the Delaware River and New Amsterdam, while England sent settlers to America by the hundreds.

Unlike most of the other colonies, the Swedish and Dutch settlements on the Delaware River did not have the guidance and encouragement of strong founders or governors. The men sent to be in charge of New Sweden were second-rate administrators who received almost no help from their sponsoring company back home. The Dutch governors were underlings sent from New Amsterdam, and under the Dutch rule the struggling little colony did not even have a name of its own, being considered simply an appendage of New Netherlands.

The colonists, therefore, developed an independence that was unthought of in colonies with strong governors. They did not hesitate to complain, as they had done to Governor Printz when they did not like his high-handed manner.

From England's point of view, the Dutch were intruders. New Netherlands separated the English shipping colonies of New England from the tobacco colonies to the south and furnished Dutch ships with a handy port. Although England tried to impose strict laws on her colonies, forbidding them to trade with anyone else, Dutch ships openly flouted these laws and took trade from Massachusetts to Virginia.

The English had already fought one brief commercial war with the Dutch from 1652 to 1654, and by 1663 she was ready to fight again. Charles II of England wanted to see the entire coast of America in the possession of the English. The two small Dutch settlements at New Amsterdam and on the Delaware River were a constant irritation to him.

To solve the problem, King Charles granted his brother, the Duke of York, a large part of what is now the State of Maine and all the

Charles II granting the New Netherlands to the Duke of York.

land between the west side of the Connecticut River and the east side of Delaware Bay (part of modern Connecticut and New York and all of modern New Jersey). The grant meant nothing so long as the Dutch still ruled the territory. The English must take it by force of arms and put English governors over it. England did not want to declare war against Holland, however, so the Duke of York sent Richard Nicolls with two war vessels to take New Netherlands.

Another Change of Names

Nicolls sailed from Massachusetts down the coast to Connecticut, where Governor Winthrop joined him. He cast anchor a short distance south of New Amsterdam, and Governor Peter Stuyvesant sent a messenger to find out the cause of the visit.

Nicolls replied, as Stuyvesant had done eight years before when he attacked the Swedes at Fort Christina, that the Dutch were trespassers on English territory and that he was there to demand that they surrender all forts and towns in the name of Charles II, King of England. Stuyvesant was as surprised as Governor Johan Rising had been, but he was not much better prepared to defend his colony. After a week of swearing and dickering back and forth with Nicolls, Governor Stuyvesant reluctantly surrendered New Amsterdam on August 27, 1664.

The fall of New Amsterdam did not mean that the colony on the Delaware River had succumbed, however. Nicolls sent his subordinate, Sir Robert Carr, down the coast, and on September 30, 1664 Carr demanded the surrender of New Amstel to the English. The fort was in no condition to defend itself, but D'Hinoyossa lost his head and defied the English. Carr fired into the little fort, wounding half of the twenty Dutch soldiers and killing three. D'Hinoyossa surrendered.

The English conquerers plundered the town and the fort. All the soldiers and many of the citizens of New Amstel were captured and sold as slaves in Virginia. They took one hundred sheep, thirty or forty horses, fifty to sixty cows and oxen. They also plundered the Mennonite village at Lewes, leaving, in the words of one resident, "not even a naile." Governor Stuyvesant in his report of the capture also said that "although the citizens of New Amstel made no resistance, they were stripped and utterly plundered."

Sir Robert Carr, however, told a different story in his report. He wrote:

> Nothing was to be had on the Delaware but what was purchased from other places, and that to supply the wants of the garrison [I] had to send into Maryland some negroes belonging to D'Hinoyossa, which [I] sold for beef, pork and salt and other small conveniences which the place affordeth not.

The Swedes, Finns, and Dutch living on the Delaware became English subjects. Most of them remained in the colony. Now that it was under English rule, colonists seeking new land came from Virginia, Maryland, New Jersey, and New York, where much of the cleared land was already taken.

Colonel Richard Nicolls, by now deputy governor of New York, visited New Amstel in October of 1664 and changed its name to New Castle. Some historians believe that he named the town for William Cavendish, the Earl of Newcastle. Others maintain that he chose the name in honor of Newcastle-upon-Tyne, a town in England that had a similar setting. Whichever designation Colonel Nicolls had in mind, the town has kept the name of New Castle to this day.

The seat of government of the Duke of York's territory remained on the Hudson River in what had been New Amsterdam, now called New York. All power, legislative and executive, was in the hands of the Duke's appointed governor. He in turn named a subordinate called a sheriff to govern the colony on the Delaware. English rule, by comparison with Dutch, was mild. The duke introduced trial by jury and allowed any Dutch soldiers who wished to remain in the colony to have fifty acres each to settle on. He made no religious restrictions. But York was narrow by nature and regarded the settlers as his subjects, whose chief purpose in life was to serve him and make him rich. Arbitrary taxes were laid on exports and imports, and the rulers in New York were rigid.

The Long Finn's Rebellion

The new English governor turned out to be no better than the Swedish and Dutch governors, and the people became depressed over their poverty. When they heard rumors that Swedish ships were on the way to recapture the colony, three men decided to do something about the oppression. Marcus Jacobsen, who was known as the Long Finn because of his height, was one of the first men in America to rebel against what he considered despotic authority. The Long Finn found supporters in John Coleman and Pastor Lars Lock, and together they spoke in taverns, churches, or anywhere else they could find a group of people gathered together. Pastor Lock used his own pulpit to expound the Long Finn's ideas of freedom, and John Coleman gathered guns, powder, and shot enough to outfit a private army.

The Long Finn called a big meeting in a tavern, and when everyone was beginning to get drunk, he mounted a table and began to arouse the people. A man who was pro-English ran out the door and called the English troops. The Long Finn was jailed, and his action was called treason by the English authorities in the colony. When word reached the governor in New York, he demanded that both Coleman and the Long Finn stand trial.

John Coleman escaped, leaving a large estate which was confiscated to the king's use. The Long Finn was taken to New York in irons. A trial was held on October 18, 1669, with the governor, Sir Francis Lovelace, presiding. Thomas Delaval and Ralph Whitfield acted as his counselors, and Thomas Willet was secretary. These four men, acted as prosecutors, judges, and jury. They promptly decided that the Long Finn was guilty of treason and inciting a rebellion, for which the penalty was death.

However, the officials were afraid that, if they hanged the leader, his followers might rise, and they would have more trouble on their hands. They therefore ordered that the Long Finn should be severely whipped and branded on his cheek with the letter "R" to show that he was a rebel. After this punishment was administered, he was kept in the jail in New York until a ship sailed for the Barbados Islands, where he was sold as a slave.

England and Holland were at war again, and the Dutch defeated the fleets of both England and her ally, France, in European waters. On the American coast a little squadron of Dutch ships under the command of Admiral Cornelis Evertsen, badly damaged the English and French trade from Newfoundland to Barbados. In August 1673 Admiral Evertsen sailed into the harbor at New York, fired his cannon, and ordered the town to surrender. The English flag came down, and once again the Dutch flag flew over New Netherlands.

A few days later he repeated the ceremony at New Castle, and for more than a year the Dutch again ruled the colony on the Delaware. By this time it made little difference to the settlers who their governors were, but one thing of importance took place during this short Dutch rule. Governor Anthony Colve established three district courts in the colony, at Uplands (modern Chester, Pennsylvania), New Castle, and Lewes. These courts eventually became the foundations for the three counties of the colony. Later, the lower county at Lewes was divided into two counties, and Chester became a part of Pennsylvania. For a while the counties were called New Castle, Jones, and Deal, before they arrived at the present designations of Kent, Sussex, and New Castle. For more than one hundred years the colony on the Delaware River had no name other than the Three Lower Counties or, occasionally, the Territory on the Delaware.

By the Treaty of Westminster, February 19, 1674, New Netherlands was restored to the English. In October of that year Major Edmund Andros arrived at New York to be the new governor of what is now New York, Pennsylvania, Delaware, and New Jersey. He sent two assistants to New Castle.

For the next six years the settlers on the Delaware lived comfortably but not luxuriously. In the forty years of the settlement they had worked hard and had built successful farms. The women still made most of the clothes, and a Swedish man could cut down a dozen two-foot-thick oak trees in a day—or so a visitor to the colony reported.

The rivers were still filled with fish and oysters, and the surrounding forest provided game in turkeys and venison. Cattle ran wild in the woods, and most of the fields grew rye for bread. Each family had its own vegetable garden and orchard. Twice a year the migrating water-fowl returned to fill the marshes and creeks. Two visitors to New Castle wrote in their journal:

> We must not forget to mention the great number of wild geese we saw here in the river. . . . There was such an incessant clatter-ing made with their wings upon the water where they rose, and such a noise of those flying higher up, that it was as if we were all the time surrounded by a whirlwind or a storm.

CHAPTER SIX

William Penn's Holy Experiment

W hen Martin Luther defied the Church of Rome and established a separate Christian church, he set the precedent for hundreds of other men to do the same thing. In 1648 an Englishman, George Fox, started a group that he called the Society of Friends. By 1654 about sixty followers were holding meetings of Friends in London, Norwich, Bristol, Wales, and elsewhere in England.

Although the Church of England was the only official church in England, the Friends held their own meetings in defiance of the law. They often attacked the "steeple houses," as they called churches, disrupting the services and taking over the pulpit to preach their own beliefs. Many of them were put in jail for this, because these beliefs differed sharply from those of the other Protestant Christians of that day.

The Friends refused to take oaths to the government, pay tithes, or obey laws that they thought were wrong. Because they believed that all men were equal in the sight of God, they refused to take off their hats as a mark of respect, even to the king. Likewise, they refused to use "you," then considered a formal form of the second person, which acknowledged that the person addressed was one's superior. They employed the familiar "thee" and "thou" for everyone. They believed Christian baptism to be a spiritual act and not one needing water. They did not believe in paying tithes for the support of a minister but maintained that the ministry was a free gift from God and that women as well as men might qualify. Outsiders nicknamed the Friends "Quakers" because they were said to quake or tremble when the Inner Light, which they called God, spoke to them.

William Penn first heard one of the Friends preach near his Irish home in 1656 when he was about twelve years old. As he grew older, he became more and more interested in the Society of Friends. He adopted its philosophy and was several times imprisoned for his speaking and pamphlet writing.

Not only were the Friends persecuted in Europe, but in America also they were driven out of several colonies or not allowed to enter them. In New England the Puritans made laws against "the cursed sect of heretics lately risen up in the world, which are commonly called Quakers." Captains of ships bringing them in were to be fined or imprisoned. Quaker books, or "writings containing their devilish opinions," were banned. Quakers themselves were sent to the house of correction, where they were severely whipped.

When Penn's father died, the government owed him a large sum of money, which he had lent to King Charles. Instead of money, William Penn asked the king to grant him a tract of land in America north of Maryland with the Delaware River on its east. King Charles agreed and gave Penn absolute power to make laws and govern as he saw fit so long as he conformed to English law.

Penn wanted to name his colony Sylvania, but King Charles insisted on naming it Pennsylvania in honor of Penn's father, a naval hero. William Penn was afraid that people would think he had named the colony for himself, so he offered the writer of the charter a bribe of twenty guineas if he would leave off the Penn, using only the name Sylvania. The man, however, dared not offend the king, so the charter, granted March 4, 1681, bears the name "Pennsylvania" heavily underscored in red ink.

The purpose of Pennsylvania—called by Penn his Holy Experiment —was to provide a refuge for Quakers and men of all other religions, and to prove that the arts and industries would thrive in such an atmosphere of benevolence. He appointed three commissioners to go to Pennsylvania to choose the site of the first town. With them went their families and about one hundred other families of colonists.

When the ships arrived in the Delaware River on December 11, 1681, they sailed upriver past the towns of New Castle and Christina as far as where Chester is now. Seeing some houses, they went ashore. That night the river froze, and the new colonists remained there all winter, many of them living in caves.

During that winter and the spring of 1682, William Penn worked on the government of his new colony. After much conferring with friends and liberal leaders, Penn drew up a constitution that allowed freedom of speech, freedom of worship, and trial by jury, by far the most liberal governing charter in any of the colonies.

Boundary Disputes

Even before the first settlement on the Delaware River, boundaries on the peninsula had been a source of dispute. When Dutch traders and explorers first sailed into the river, the English governors of Virginia charged them with trespassing.

The kings, who so willingly made grants of thousands of acres of land either to pay off debts or as gifts to favorites, knew nothing of the country they were giving away. Only a few crude maps had yet been made of the seacoast, and no one knew how far west the land extended. Moreover, political realities being what they were, one monarch might easily overrule grants made by his predecessors and issue new charters, superseding the old.

In this fashion the land along the west bank of the Delaware River was granted for colonization over and over. It was included in the original grant of Virginia, which extended from latitude 34 to 45 degrees north. Lord Baltimore received a grant from King Charles I for territory "hitherto unsettled" extending from the mouth of the Potomac River as far north as the 40th parallel. This grant included the land on the west bank of the Delaware River.

However, the Dutch colony at Zwaanendael had been settled in 1631, a year before the Maryland charter was issued. Therefore, lawyers for the Dutch pointed out that Lord Baltimore's grant did not apply to the west bank of the river. Baltimore's answer was that that first settlement, at Zwaanendael, had been wiped out before Maryland was settled. (Indeed, many Delawareans still consider New Sweden, 1638, their first settlement.)

61

The quarrel between Lord Baltimore and the Dutch was well known in England, and if the issue had been fought out in the courts at that time, Lord Baltimore would doubtless have sustained his case against the Dutch West India Company. But it was allowed to slide, and in 1664, when the Duke of York wanted to attach the colony on the Delaware to his claim of New York, King Charles gave his consent. When the duke sent his commissioners to take charge of the territory, he told them that Baltimore's title was very doubtful.

Lord Baltimore objected strenuously to this, but since the Duke of York's control of the Delaware was by the consent of the king, he knew that his protests would receive little attention at court. But then William Penn entered the picture.

The Twelve Mile Circle

According to Pennsylvania's charter, her southern border was to start "from the beginning of the fortieth degree of North Latitude." At the time the charter was drawn, it was thought that the 40th degree ran about twelve miles north of New Castle (actually it runs through the site of Philadelphia), so a circle was drawn, the courthouse of New Castle being the center, twelve miles in radius. This circle, still visible on modern maps, was to be the boundary between York's territory on the Delaware and Penn's colony of Pennsylvania.

Pennsylvania was the largest land grant ever made to a private citizen anywhere in the world—larger than the whole of Ireland. But this vast territory did not have easy access to the sea, or so it seemed to Penn. He wanted to control the mouth of the Delaware. So he asked the Duke of York to make a further grant to him.

York had served in the navy with Penn's father and felt a liking for him. So in August 1682 he granted Penn the town of New Castle and the Twelve Mile Circle, plus a tract of land south to Cape Henlopen.

Actually, York had no legal title to the land himself, because the king had never given him a formal grant. So, the following March he obtained a patent for New Castle and the Twelve Mile Circle and handed them over to Penn. A month later, he surrendered his March

The Old Court House in New Castle was built at various times during two hundred years. The center section was built first and the two wings were added about 1765. The spire of the Court House was used as the center of the circle for the Twelve Mile Circle.

grant and requested a new one for all of the west bank of the Delaware. And a month after that, Penn himself petitioned for a grant of Delaware. It was still pending in 1685 when Charles II died and the Duke of York became King James II. James promptly sidestepped a long legal wrangle and granted the land directly to Penn. This time the grant stuck.

Oddly enough, James never did convey title to the region to Penn on paper. This led to many quarrels later when the collectors of quitrents from Pennsylvania tried to force the citizens in Delaware to pay.

No one knows why the Twelve Mile Circle was not ignored after James agreed to grant Penn the Three Lower Counties, or why it was not replaced by a straight line when they became a state, but the Twelve Mile Circle remains today the northern boundary of the State of Delaware.

The New Proprietor

In October 1682, while title to Delaware was still unsettled, the *Welcome* sailed into the harbor at New Castle, bringing William Penn in person. The new governor of the Three Lower Counties presented his agreements with James, Duke of York, to John Moll and Ephraim Herman, two magistrates who held the power of attorney from the duke. They conducted the ceremony of transferring the Three Lower Counties to the governorship of William Penn. Penn entered the fort alone, locked the door, and opened it again. Then he was presented with a porringer of river water and soil with a twig laid upon it—symbols of his sovereignty. This ceremony, called the livery of seizin, was followed by a mass swearing of allegiance by the colonists.

These colonists had not had a name of their own since New Sweden days, and they offered no objection to becoming a part of Pennsylvania.

William Penn arrives at New Castle on October 27, 1682, to be greeted by the ceremony of livery of seizin. Ceremonially, Penn entered the town fort alone, locked the door, and opened it again, at which time he was presented with a porringer of river water and soil with a twig upon it.

Penn sailed on up the river to view the site for his new settlement, which he named Philadelphia, from the Greek words *philos* and *adelphos*, meaning "brotherly love."

When Lord Baltimore heard that King Charles and the Duke of York had given William Penn the land on the west bank of the Delaware, he decided to confront Penn with the matter. He invited the governor of the Friends' colony to come to Maryland. In December of 1682 Penn set out with William Markham, his cousin and deputy governor, and several other Friends to meet Lord Baltimore at the house of Colonel Thomas Tailler in Anne Arundel County, Maryland.

It was the boundary of Pennsylvania that they argued about first. Lord Baltimore insisted on 40 degrees north as Penn's southern boundary (as, indeed, both their charters stated) and wanted to fix the degree by celestial observation. But Penn was just as obstinate, claiming that the term "beginning of the fortieth degree" gave him some latitude in determining his boundaries. Since his charter entitled his colony to a breadth of two degrees, the same as Maryland's, he wanted to decide where they lay by measuring the degrees on the ground. And he wanted Maryland to start measuring her two degrees some miles inside Virginia.

Penn's object was to obtain an outlet on Chesapeake Bay in addition to what he already had on the Delaware. However, it was Penn's control of the Three Lower Counties that really irritated Baltimore. He reminded Penn that the Quaker had promised him once in England that he would not try to get this land, but Penn evaded the point. Penn left Maryland without reaching any agreement with Lord Baltimore.

The two proprietors met again in May 1683 at New Castle, but still no agreement was reached. Following this meeting each man wrote a lengthy letter to influential persons in England, setting forth his position and asking for favor.

Finally, Penn and Baltimore both went to England to present their claims to the Lords of Trade and Plantations. Penn's lawyers pointed out the two Latin words in Baltimore's grant—*hactenus inculta*, meaning "previously uncultivated." Since the Dutch colony of Zwaanendael had been settled before the Maryland grant, the Lords of Trade and Plantations decided that "the territory along the Delaware had been

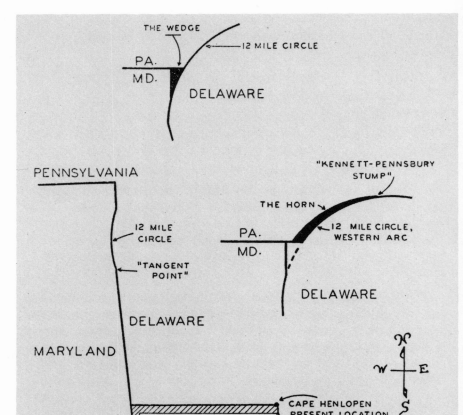

THE WEDGE

12 MILE CIRCLE

PA.
MD.

DELAWARE

PENNSYLVANIA

"KENNETT-PENNSBURY
STUMP"

THE HORN

12 MILE
CIRCLE

PA.
MD.

12 MILE CIRCLE,
WESTERN ARC

"TANGENT
POINT"

DELAWARE

DELAWARE

MARYLAND

N
W — E
S

CAPE HENLOPEN
PRESENT LOCATION

AREA IN DISPUTE IN
PENN VS. LORD BALTIMORE

"MIDDLE POINT"

FENWICK'S ISLAND APPEARING
AS CAPE HENLOPEN ON MAP
ANNEXED TO ARTICLES OF 1732.

MASON AND DIXON SURVEY — FROM MIDDLE POINT NORTH AS
INDICATED AND THENCE WEST TO FORM MARYLAND–PENNSYLVANIA LINE,
THE SO-CALLED MASON AND DIXON LINE.

This drawing is not accurate to scale, but it shows the area in dispute between
the Penns and Lord Baltimore because of the mistake of calling what is now
Fenwick's Island Cape Henlopen on early maps.

settled by Christians antecedently to his [Baltimore's] grant and was therefore not included in it."

As a compromise, the lawyers agreed that the peninsula between Delaware Bay and Chesapeake Bay should be divided north and south from the latitude of Cape Henlopen into equal parts. The eastern half was to belong to Penn and the western half to Maryland. The Three Lower Counties finally had their borders defined, although another eighty years would pass before they were determined permanently.

CHAPTER SEVEN

Growth and Conflict

The founding of Pennsylvania brought the greatest activity the Delaware River had ever known. In the first three years seven thousand immigrants sailed into the river. While most of them settled in the vicinity of Philadelphia, many spread out into the Swedish-Dutch towns down the river.

The new settlers brought with them a higher standard of living and more modern ideas of agriculture than the original settlers knew. Competition with them stimulated the people who had lived there for two generations, and they tried to produce more than they had before. Soon they were exporting meat, grain, flour, bread, barrel staves, lumber, and horses as well as the usual tobacco and skins. Most of these products were shipped to the West Indies, where the planters found it profitable to buy their food from the colonies in America in exchange for sugar, molasses, rum, salt, and Negroes. Shipping became the most important industry on the Delaware River.

A Separate Assembly

Although William Penn had not rested until he acquired the Three Lower Counties from James, once he had established Philadelphia, he gave it all of his attention. The little counties spread out for one hundred miles down the Delaware River were a part of Pennsylvania and a protection for Philadelphia, but Penn wasted no time trying to develop them.

The Assembly met in Philadelphia, and each county sent six representatives to it. From 1682, when Penn arrived at New Castle and presented his deeds until 1704, the people of the Three Lower Counties accepted this form of government. Many of the men who were interested in politics sold their land on the peninsula and moved to Philadelphia, attracted by the excitement of a bustling city. Others kept their homes in the Three Lower Counties, but moved their businesses or offices to Philadelphia.

By the time Penn took over the colony, the Swedes and Dutch were already outnumbered by the English. The original settlers preferred life on the farm and were content to let the English run the affairs of government. The names of a few of these early politicians appear in the records of the colony from time to time but no strong leadership had formed.

Although Penn was more lenient in his charter of the government of Pennsylvania than most royal governors, the people of the Three Lower Counties felt that, since they had been managing their own affairs for many years before Penn arrived, they were perfectly capable of continuing to do so. Furthermore, although the Duke of York had granted Penn a deed to the land along the Delaware River, he had made no mention of the government of the people who lived there.

Later, when Penn's right to govern the Three Lower Counties was challenged, the Privy Council decided that, although Penn was free to rule Pennsylvania as he pleased, his claim to Delaware was not so absolute. He might appoint the same man to be governor of both colonies, but the Delaware half of the appointment had to have the king's consent. Throughout its history as a separate colony, Delaware remained in a queer position politically—half proprietorial, half royal.

Men used this argument to promote a schism between the Pennsylvania government in Philadelphia and that of the Three Lower Counties. They felt that the latter should be in an independent position. At the same time, they also knew that Delaware was not strong enough or wealthy enough to govern itself completely. So, for twenty-two years after Penn took over the territory, the people submitted to his rule, all the while objecting to and protesting against restrictions on their independence.

Lord Baltimore also played a part in unifying the residents of the

Three Lower Counties against Penn. He continuously sent agents into the counties to stir up ill feelings. At a meeting of the Assembly on February 1, 1684, a representative from the Lower Counties reported that most of the people of Kent County were ready to revolt because Governor Penn had not kept a promise to clear all ships entering and leaving the river at New Castle. He added that should they secede, Lord Baltimore had promised to help them.

By 1690 jealousies had increased. The Lower Counties insisted that they were not being treated fairly in the appointment of offices. Without telling the president of the Assembly in Philadelphia, several local officials met secretly and appointed six judges. When the Assembly learned of this, they declared the appointments illegal.

Things rocked along until 1701. At this time the king asked Penn to raise £350 from his colony to help maintain the fortifications at New York. When Penn passed this request along to the Assembly, the members from the Three Lower Counties protested that they did not have enough funds to protect themselves, much less to help New York.

Another disagreement arose later that year, when the Assembly in Philadelphia insisted on confirming several decisions made by the Delaware representatives at a meeting they had formerly held at New Castle. The men of the Three Lower Counties stated in a protest that their union with Pennsylvania asserted that they were to have equal rights with the upper counties in all things and that their Assembly meeting at New Castle was just as legal as the one in Philadelphia—hence its decisions did not need confirming.

William Penn was greatly hurt by this dissension, but before he left for England he added a proviso to the charter stating: "If the representatives of the province and territories shall not hereafter agree to join together in legislation . . . I do hereby promise, grant and declare, that the inhabitants of both province and territories shall separately enjoy all other liberties, privileges, and benefits granted jointly to them, in this charter."

The Three Lower Counties were granted three years to see if they could get along with the upper counties, but matters continued to grow worse, and in April 1704 the Three Lower Counties were given their

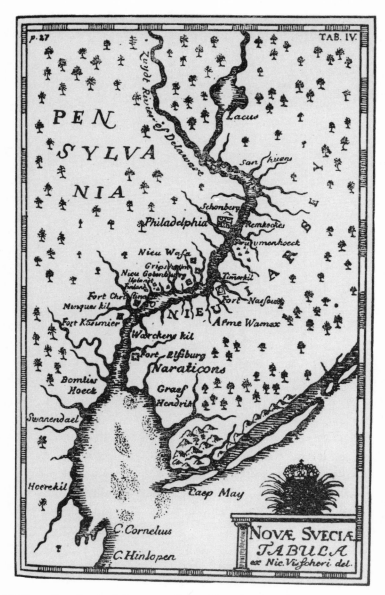

By 1700 New Sweden had been swallowed by the Dutch, then by the English.
William Penn had become proprietor of the Three Lower Counties, and Philadelphia had already grown to be larger than New Castle. But the country is
still called New Sweden in this book published in Stockholm in 1702.

own Assembly. They were still a part of Pennsylvania but now had the independence to make laws which would pertain to their special needs rather than those of Philadelphia.

The first Assembly of the Three Lower Counties met in November 1704, and most of the same men who had been representatives to the Assembly in Philadelphia were reelected. After gaining this unprecedented independence from their governor, the Assembly of the Three Lower Counties did little to strengthen their position or try to become a separate colony. For the next sixty years their lives flowed gently from year to year with no events which the Assembly saw fit to record. In fact, few records were kept of meetings, and the journals of the Assembly before the year 1762 were not even preserved.

Quakers Versus Pirates

Delaware's long coastline had been prey to piratical raids for many years. In the days of Dutch supremacy, Governor Peter Stuyvesant—no man to be trifled with—gathered a fleet of yachts (originally *jachtschiff*, "hunting ship," a light, swift pursuit vessel) and sent them to patrol the coast of New Netherlands, watching for pirates. When the yachtsmen caught such freebooters, they hanged the rascals then and there. Forced out of their New York territory, the pirates moved down the coast to the mouth of the Delaware, where they engaged in new depredations.

In 1685 King James II of England, the former Duke of York, sent ships to defend the Delaware coast. He offered a pardon to any pirate who would give himself up, pay a fine, and settle down to live as a citizen. Some of the pirates did give themselves up, but instead of a pardon, they were jailed or hanged. The wealthy—that is, successful—pirates simply bribed officials and continued their harassment.

The Delaware River was not a favorite haunt of pirates, because the shoals and currents of the bay made a fast getaway difficult, but raids were made on New Castle and Lewes from time to time. The pirates brought terror to the citizens of these towns, preyed on ships in the bay, and plundered the homes near the shore. They are said to have buried treasure on many of Delaware's sandy beaches.

The citizens of the Three Lower Counties wanted to protect themselves against such depredations and felt that a strong local militia, which could be quickly assembled in an emergency, would be their best defense. But the Quakers who had settled in the region refused to provide their share of money and men to such a defense force. Pacifism was basic to their beliefs, and they considered fighting, even for self-protection, an abomination. They were backed up by the Assembly in Philadelphia, which was dominated by Quakers and, being farther up the river, felt less threatened by piracy.

The people of the more exposed regions complained to the governor of Pennsylvania of their lack of protection, but he, too, was often a Quaker. Consequently, the Delaware coast went undefended.

As might have been predicted, pirates went happily on with their sea robbery. In their time Blackbeard, Avery, and Blueskin all visited Delaware. On a September afternoon in 1698 a small sloop anchored offshore near Lewes. Next morning Captain Canoot and fifty well-armed men landed and sacked the town. Methodically they plundered every house, taking with them all the money, jewels, clothes, and silver they found. They killed hogs, sheep, and chickens, and forced several men of the town to help them carry their booty to the sloop and stow it. Taking with them the town carpenter as a prisoner—carpenters and surgeons were nearly always impressed by pirates, who needed their skills—they sailed jauntily out of the harbor. No one pursued.

In April of 1700 the famous Captain William Kidd paid one of his visits to the Delaware. On this occasion he anchored some distance from the coast and sent word to Lewes that his ship was loaded with rare treasures from the Orient. (It was, too—he had taken them from a fine Armenian ship off Madagascar.) Several prominent citizens of the town rowed out to the ship and purchased a large part of his plunder, although there were laws prohibiting trade with pirates.

Kidd went on to New York and later London's Execution Dock, but he left behind memories. It is said that the village of Kitts Hummock was originally called Kidd's Hammock, perhaps because his anchorage was nearby. And rumors persist that every once in a while, after a storm or very high tide, an ancient coin may be washed up on the beach.

Kidd at least did not try to raid the American continent, but others who had gone "on the account" were not so particular, and the raids continued well into the eighteenth century. Many men, otherwise perfectly honest, made no bones about dealing with pirates, fitting out their ships or buying their ill-gotten merchandise. Even William Markham, Penn's deputy, was suspected of trading with pirates. When he retired, many people said it was because he had been caught buying and selling stolen goods.

Nevertheless the Quakers remained adamant against providing protection. Once, although there was no sign of a pirate attack, the officials of Lewes thought they would test out the Quakers. They sent a man on horseback up the coast to Philadelphia to report that a pirate ship was on its way up the river to attack the city.

He rode up to the governor's office in great haste and poured out his message. If the Quakers would fight to defend the town, he urged, they could drive the pirates away.

Instead, the Quakers stuck to their principles. Many fled to the country, taking whatever valuables they could gather up. Others, unable to flee, resolved to make the best of it. They threw their silver into the well or quickly buried it, and then braced themselves for the "raid." No one offered to defend the town.

This conflict went on into the 1740's, when better naval protection at last made piracy too dangerous a trade.

CHAPTER EIGHT

Towns

M eanwhile, the towns of the Three Lower Counties began to grow. The increased population and activity, due to their closeness to Philadelphia, was the chief reason. Lewes developed into a fair-sized port, which shipped grain, meat, and timber for ships. Being the southernmost town on Delaware Bay, it became the home of the river pilots who boarded each ship that entered the river to guide it through the shoals and sandbars up to Philadelphia.

Just south of Lewes, Rehoboth was named by a group of English settlers about 1675. It is said to mean "room enough," and to have been named from a biblical passage, Genesis 26:22: "And he removed from thence, and digged another well; and for that they strove not: and he called the name of it Rehoboth; and he said, For now the Lord hath made room for us, and we shall be fruitful in the land."

The land was divided into plantations, and gradually larger and larger fields of corn, tobacco, flax, wheat, and other crops surrounded the cypress-board plantation houses with their slave quarters.

Farther north and a few miles inland where Milford now stands, a few large farms and plantations covered most of the countryside near the Mispillion River. North Milford, the older part of the town, stands on a tract formerly called Saw Mill Range, owned by Henry Bowman.

Before 1680 the land around what is now Dover was a part of Sussex County, but in that year it was divided and named St. Jones County. The name was later changed to Kent. The site of the town, which is now the capital of the state, was part of an estate of eight hundred acres owned by two brothers and called the Brothers' Portion. They

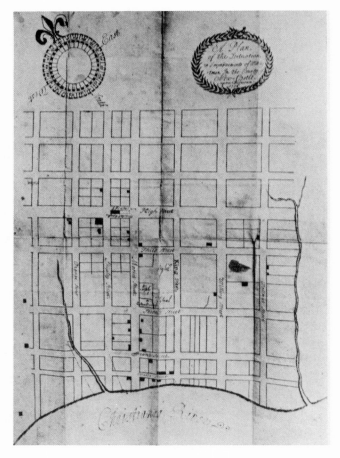

Most of the land along Christina River was owned by a few men who handed it down to their children, so that little of it was sold. Andrew Justison managed to purchase a parcel of land, however, and about 1730 he decided to lay it out in tracts for a town. His Willington eventually became Wilmington.

bought it from the Indians for three coats, twelve bottles of rum, and four handfuls of powder.

New Castle had far outgrown Christina, and the few remaining Swedes who still lived in the original little town on The Rocks went about their business quietly. About 1690, Andrew Printz, a nephew of the former governor, visited Christina. He saw that the Swedes needed books and clergymen, so when he went home he told his story to several friends and finally it reached King Charles XI. The king sent three ministers to Christina in 1697. One of them, Eric Bjorck, stayed in the town while the other two went elsewhere.

All the land around Christina was held by only a few landowners. Two men between them owned all the land from the Christina River to Brandywine Creek and from The Rocks to Rattlesnake Run. A Dutch settler owned most of the land across the Brandywine and across the Christina was a farm that belonged to Jean Paul Jaquet, who had been the first Dutch director at Fort Casimir. Most men handed down their land to their widows and children, so that little of it was sold, making it hard for new settlers to invade the country around Christina.

Andrew Justison was one of the few outsiders who were able to purchase a parcel of land. About 1730 he had his land surveyed and laid out in tracts for a town, beginning at the present French Street of Wilmington and extending along the Christina Creek to West Street and north to Third Street. It was to be a farmers' town with services for ships and mills. Justison set aside free ground for a marketplace for the farmers and built a ropewalk and sail loft. He sold a few lots, but no one seemed interested in helping him build his town.

In 1734 Justison's daughter Catherine married Thomas Willing. Thomas went into business with his father-in-law and tried to sell lots in the new town, but his efforts also failed, and the plan was abandoned. However, they changed the name of the town from Christina to Willingtown.

A Quaker's Dream Come True

About this same time, an energetic young woman named Elizabeth Lewis, who was a minister of the Friends in Pennsylvania, married a man named William Shipley. Elizabeth was a fervent missionary and believed strongly in guidance through dreams. One night she dreamed that with a guide she was making a ministerial journey on horseback into an unknown country. Riding to the top of a high hill she saw a lovely valley, through which ran a river. On the banks of the river were a few settlers' cabins.

Elizabeth's guide told her that it was a new settlement and that it would grow to become a large and prosperous city. He also said that divine Providence had guided her to the place and that, if she and her family would move there, they would be blessed by Heaven for their efforts.

When the young woman awoke, she was greatly impressed with her dream and told her husband every detail of it, describing the country exactly. William Shipley told his wife that he did not intend to leave his well-established life in Pennsylvania and move to some undeveloped fairyland.

Several years later, Elizabeth set out on a journey similar to the one about which she had dreamed. She rode down the peninsula from Pennsylvania to visit some Friends. As she crossed Brandywine Creek on the old ford above the Great Falls and climbed the hill above it, she came out into a little clearing near a Swedish log cabin. When she looked down into the valley, she was astonished to see the very landscape about which she had dreamed.

In great excitement Elizabeth returned home to tell William Shipley. After much persuasion he agreed to go with her to see the country she had described. William was a very practical and shrewd businessman, and when he saw the location of Willingtown on the Brandywine he realized that its rushing stream offered great power for mills. He immediately bought a lot on Second Street.

In that spring of 1735 the little town had only fifteen to twenty houses. William Shipley returned in August and bought the entire town west of Market Street. That fall he brought Elizabeth and his family from Pennsylvania. The Shipleys lived in a small brick house on Fourth Street, between Shipley and Orange Streets. Later they built a mansion at the corner of Fourth and Shipley Streets.

William Shipley and his wife were both influential and wealthy Friends. When they first moved to Willingtown, they were the only Friends there, and the natives called them Quakers. Soon many of their friends moved in, bought the new houses which Shipley built, and started businesses. The number of houses doubled in the first year after the Shipleys moved there, and the community became known as a Quaker town.

The "Upstart Village"

Although Shipley was more interested in other industries than he was in farming, he quickly recognized the necessity of having the farmers come to town to sell their produce to the people in the industries. Ignoring the free land given to the town by Willing on which to build a market, Shipley built a large market on his own property. Willing had been unable to build a market house on his land, because he could not get enough people to subscribe funds for it and lacked the money to do it himself.

As soon as Shipley's market was in business, however, many of the older families protested the building of a privately owned market. Since the town was not incorporated, it had no formal government, and

Although Wilmington was mainly a Quaker town, the First Presbyterian Church was built there in 1740. It has since been removed from the original site and the building is now used as a meeting place for the Colonial Dames.

now that they were divided over the market, some way must be found to reconcile the dispute.

Both Willing and Shipley appealed to Thomas Penn, who was then proprietor of the Three Lower Counties. After much squabbling eighty-two subscribers made up enough money to buy Shipley's market and make it public. Not to be outdone, the older families raised enough money to build a bigger and more handsome market on the land that Willing had set aside.

The town now asked Penn for a charter, and when it was drawn up, in November 1739, it provided that in the future, sites for markets and days for their being open would be decided by vote of those citizens who paid an annual rent of five pounds or more. As the result of the first vote, Shipley's market was open on Saturdays and was the site of the spring fair. Willing's market was open on Wednesday and was the site of the fall fair.

The market dispute was probably the cause of Shipley's changing the name of the town from Willingtown to Wilmington. The two names were enough alike to be the same thing, but Shipley considered the town his and wanted to be the one who named it. He chose the name Wilmington in honor of the Penns' friend, Spencer Compton, Earl of Wilmington, whose only claim to association with the town was through the issuing of the charter.

At the first election of officers under the new charter William Shipley was named chief burgess. Under his direction the town grew rapidly, and that same year Shipley, with several other prominent men as partners, built a brig named the *Wilmington*. When the *Wilmington* sailed down the Delaware River loaded with flour, beef, butter, and lumber, William Shipley set up competition with New Castle, which had been the shipping port for the Three Lower Counties. The next ten years brought about a change in status for both towns. New Castle was soon described as suffering a wretched fate and being in a dying condition owing to an "upstart village" lying on a neighboring creek.

Elizabeth Shipley's dream had come true. Most of the Quakers were shrewd business people as well as hard-working and industrious. At the same time, their beliefs gave both men and women a freedom of thought and expression which other religions deliberately sought to stifle. Under the liberal political government of Pennsylvania, the Quakers had nothing to hold them back. Whenever they chose a location like that of Wilmington, which was already blessed with natural resources, they set to work to make it the most prosperous place in the area, often to the jealousy of surrounding inhabitants and towns.

Quakers had different values of right and wrong from those of other people. Abominating war as they did, they channeled their energies into commerce and industry instead, and often this made them wealthy men. As the *Wilmington* voyaged to and from the West Indies, William Shipley and his partners grew rich from the profits of the cargoes of rum, sugar, and molasses. One such partner withdrew from the company, because his conscience would not allow him to make such great profits. He opened his own company in Wilmington and charged lower prices than the others to cut down his own profits.

Most Quakers did not seem to be bothered by scruples in that particular fashion, but when a Quaker became rich, he was expected to contribute to charity in proportion to his wealth. The Quakers were not ones to sit by and see some men in want while others enjoyed plenty.

CHAPTER NINE

Industry on the Brandywine

When William Shipley first visited the Brandywine with his wife, it took him only one look to see the possibilities of the river. To him, the water rushing over the rock falls, where once the Indians had fished, meant power for mills.

The farmers in the surrounding flat lands grew wheat and rye, which they shipped to England to be made into flour. Early settlers built a few mills on smaller streams, but if the wheat could be milled in large amounts on the Brandywine and the flour shipped instead of the whole grain, the millers could get a better price for it, and the industry would help the economy of the whole Three Lower Counties. Nowhere on the coast of North America was there quite such waterpower quite so easily available as on the Brandywine.

In the first sixty miles upstream from tidewater, the Brandywine River falls almost a thousand feet. Only four miles upstream from Wilmington, the rivers falls 120 feet. A small Swedish barley mill was built near the old ford above the Great Falls at Wilmington as early as 1687. It was enlarged in 1727, and in 1742 it was bought and enlarged again by one Oliver Canby.

But before a mill can be built, the water to turn its wheel must be controlled, usually by means of a milldam. But the rapid flow of the water through the narrow rock gorge above Wilmington made it almost impossible to build a dam. The easiest way to channel the water was to find a ledge of rock or a rock slide like the one near where the Hagley Museum now stands. The miller could dig a short ditch called a raceway from the pool above the rapids and divert enough water through it to

Nowhere on the coast of North America was there such waterpower as on the Brandywine River. Mills sprang up all along the river near Wilmington. Conestoga wagons brought grain from Pennsylvania and Maryland as well as Delaware, and shallops sailed away loaded with flour.

Replica of a waterwheel at the Hagley Museum in Wilmington.

turn a wheel. The water ran under the wheel, turning it clockwise. This was called an undershot wheel.

Wheat into Flour

By a system of gears, the waterwheel turned a millstone inside the millhouse. The lower or bed stone was fixed permanently on the floor of the millhouse. The top stone or runner, geared to the wheel, turned slowly around on the bed stone.

The millstones were made of granite. They were about four feet in diameter and were formed of wedge-shaped pieces strongly cemented together and bound by iron hoops around the circumference. The surfaces of the stones were chiseled into a series of radiating ridges and furrows. The grain was fed into a hole in the center of the runner, and as it rotated slowly around the top of the bed stone, the grain was pushed from the center to the circumference by the ridges, being crushed into flour as it went. It was important that the two stones were perfectly level and perfectly parallel to one another, and they were made in matched pairs.

Oliver Canby was fortunate in his mill site. The bridge across the first tidewater pool was washed away, and a new bridge was built just below the Great Falls. This left the river open the entire way from his mill to the Delaware River, and the shallops could come almost to his door. Above Canby's mill the King's Road crossed a ford on its way from Philadelphia to Baltimore. Grain could be brought to his mill by wagon at the back door and shipped as flour from his front door.

By 1672 the old First Dam was built across the head of the last rapids to make a pool above. A long raceway was dug from it on the west bank of the Brandywine, and the powerful stream of water flowing down this raceway was strong enough to push an overshot wheel—a wheel which was driven by water flowing over the top. It ran clockwise and was far more efficient than an undershot wheel.

Other men saw the profit in the Brandywine's power. Joseph Tatnall, a friend of George Washington, built a raceway on the eastern side of the river, and soon at the mouth of the gorge at Wilmington there were two raceways, one above the other.

Once the old First Dam had been built and they could have their wheat ground into flour, the farmers began to clear larger and larger plantations in western Delaware and the Eastern Shore of Maryland. The wheat was of such good quality that flour made from it was shipped all over the world. It was said that one year Joseph Tatnall bought the entire crop of one plantation owner for $40,000 cash.

Unintentionally, the flour mills helped to develop a means of transportation which, like the log cabin, later became identified with the opening of the West. The Conestoga wagon was developed in Pennsylvania for hauling grain to the mills on the Brandywine River. Named after a tribe of the Minqua Indians, it was so heavy when loaded with

To provide water for overshot waterwheels, the Brandywine River was diverted into raceways alongside the main stream. This controlled stream made possible the efficient operation of the gristmills that flourished along the river.

wheat that six horses were needed to pull it. One big advantage of the Conestoga wagon was its cover. Made of canvas stretched over staves bent and fastened to the sides of the body, the cover protected the wagon's cargo from rain.

Many years later the same kind of covered wagons protected families with all their worldly possessions as they moved across the Allegheny Mountains. A smaller and lighter version of the Conestoga wagon, called the prairie schooner, crossed the continent on the Santa Fe, the California, and Oregon Trails.

Tanning

Another industry which developed about this time along the banks of the Brandywine was tanning. As the herds of cattle grew, so did the supply of hides. The skin of any animal could be made into leather, but usually the skins were from animals which had been raised and

Tanning leather was a slow process, and like roasting beef or toasting bread, it could not be hurried. This diorama at the Hagley Museum shows all the operations up to the final currying of the tanned hides.

slaughtered for some other purpose: oxen, horses, calves, sheep, and goats. Cowhide was the most popular, being tough and durable.

The skins of all animals consist of a fibrous substance called collagen. If the hide is boiled, the collagen forms gelatin. However, if the hide is treated with tannin, the collagen unites with the tannin to form an insoluble compound called tanno-gelatin, which is the basis of tanned leather.

The forests along the Brandywine were filled with oak and hemlock trees. The bark of the oak tree contains 7 to 11 percent of tannin and is one of the best barks for tanning leather. In the early days of the colonies, however, hemlock was more often used where it was more plentiful than oak.

The bark of the trees was easily removed in the spring when the sap was flowing. The trees were cut down, and the rough exterior part of the bark removed by means of a sharp instrument called a scraper. The bark was dried in sheds on frames or shelves, so that the air could circulate through it and the bark would not get moldy.

Once the bark was dried, the juice which contains the tannic acid or tannin was extracted by crushing. It could then be mixed with water in whatever amount was necessary to tan the raw leather.

Tanning leather was a slow process, and like roasting beef or toasting bread it could not be hurried. First, the hide must be cleaned and softened. This was done by working the hide under water with wooden paddles until it was soft and pliable. Next, the hides were soaked in pits of limewater to soften the hair, or sometimes they were sweated with damp heat until the hair and underskin tissues began to ferment and putrefy, making it easier to scrape off. They were then stretched over a tanner's beam, and the hair and scarf skin were removed by shaving with a fleshing knife.

The scraped hides were stacked in pits containing a mixture of water and tannic acid, called ooze, which was made increasingly strong as the hides were moved from pit to pit. In the first pits with the weak solutions, the hides were turned over several times a day, but in the last pits they were left for as much as six weeks in the ooze without being disturbed.

When they were finally taken from the tan pits, the hides were drained and covered from the light, so that the acid would not discolor them. They were then hung in a loft to dry.

When thoroughly dry, they were softened in water, then liberally oiled. The whole surface was worked over by a three-sided steel implement called a striking pin. This operation removed all creases and smoothed and solidified the leather, which was then ready to be made into shoes and other articles.

One of the greatest drawbacks of the tanning industry was the fact that, because of the fermentation and putrefaction during the processing of the skins, a tannery could be smelled many miles away when the wind was right. Most people did not want to build their homes near a tannery. Like many modern industries, tanning flourished on the Brandywine because of the available water supply, and pollution of both the water and the air was the consequence.

Papermaking

Another industry that needed water was papermaking. This industry was already old when America was discovered, and it was still made on the Brandywine as it had been for about two thousand years—by hand. A vat was filled with water into which were put vegetable fibers to make a pulp. Most often the fibers were of cloth that had been shredded into threads.

The paper was made by dipping a wooden frame the size of a sheet of paper into the vat containing the pulp. To the frame was fastened a sheet of screening that allowed the water to run out as the mold was shaken back and forth to scatter the fibers evenly over the surface of the sieve. When all the water was drained, the mass of pulp was carefully removed, pressed, and dried, making one sheet of paper.

Papermaking, tanning, and flour milling were all slow processes in the early days along the Brandywine, but because men were interested in improving their industry or making more money from it, many of the modern mechanizations in these industries took place on the river above Wilmington.

88

Although papermaking was old when America was discovered, the invention of the printing press made it an important industry in the new colonies. Paper made on the Brandywine was still made by the laborious hand process which had been used for about two thousand years.

Quaker Hill

Wilmington became a Quaker town, and despite their humility and plain dress, the Quaker men were intensely competitive and eager to get rich rapidly. The trading Quakers lived mostly on Quaker Hill, a hill above Christina Creek, where their meetinghouse was built. It was a square brick building with a truncated roof sheltering the doorway and was surrounded by solid brick houses. Like the meetinghouse, the Quaker dwellings were plain on the outside but were well designed and often luxuriously furnished inside with furniture, china, and rugs brought from Europe and the Orient.

The Quaker millers lived in the valley along the Brandywine where their mills were located. One of the first to build his home in this area was Oliver Canby, owner of the first flour mill. About 1747 he built a gracious stone house above the river, which is now the residence of the Episcopal bishop of Delaware.

The Quakers were as serious about their children's education as they were about their religion. This drawing shows the Friends' first meetinghouse in Wilmington. During the week the building was used for a school and is still a part of the present Friends' School.

The Quakers were still thought of as a peculiar people. Their beliefs did not prevent them from becoming wealthy but did demand strong disciplines. They must dress in gray or brown clothes. The men wore low-crowned, broad-brimmed hats, and the women wore scuttle bonnets. A wealthy Quaker, however, even though his clothes conformed to the prescribed colors, had them made from the finest quality of cloth available.

They called other Quakers "brother" or "sister," and since they believed that everyone was equal in the sight of God, they clung to the old usage of "thee" and "thou" without respect to their station in life. A Quaker boy, wishing to use a mild curse, which of course was forbidden, would call his fellow schoolboy, "Hey, you."

There were no poor Quakers. If a brother suffered misfortune, for instance, if his house burned down or his crop failed, the Society of Friends took care of him until he could get back on his feet again. If a man did not make money because of his character, he was thought to be no real Quaker and was "read out of meeting," which meant that he was put out of the society.

CHAPTER TEN

Boundaries, Black Men, and Indians

The boundary dispute between Lord Baltimore and William Penn continued long after both of the men were dead. When the court decided that the Delmarva Peninsula should be split down the center, many settlers who thought they were part of the Swedish-Dutch-English colony found themselves over the line in Maryland. No one knew exactly where the line ran, and frequently agents from both governments tried to collect the quitrents from the same settler.

Charles Mason and Jeremiah Dixon

The most disputed boundary now, however, was the one between Pennsylvania and Maryland. Eighty years after the founding of the Pennsylvania colony, it still was a point of contention. Neither King Charles II nor his successors had much interest in the squabble. But as time went on, the dispute became a major issue with the heirs of William Penn and Lord Baltimore and also with the people who lived within the boundaries.

At last, in 1732, Lord Baltimore gave in and agreed to allow an east-west border between him and his neighbor that was well below the 40th degree. A straight line should be run due west from a point beginning fifteen miles south of the southernmost latitude of the city of Philadelphia—39 degrees 43 minutes North latitude.

In 1750, while further court action delayed the final surveying of the border, two commissioners for Pennsylvania and two for Maryland laid out the southern boundary of the Three Lower Counties. They met at a point on the Atlantic Ocean about half way between the 38th and 39th parallels and surveyed a line that runs north of west for about thirty-five miles to the center of the peninsula, called Middle Point.

In 1763 the governments of Maryland and Pennsylvania agreed to let professionals settle the dispute once and for all. They hired two English astronomers, Charles Mason and Jeremiah Dixon, to come over and survey the lines. These two men started their work by resurveying the southern boundary between Maryland and the Three Lower Counties, to verify it. Next they started from the western end of that line, Middle Point, and ran the boundary between the Three Lower Counties and Maryland northward one hundred miles to where it intersected the Twelve Mile Circle.

In order to set up a point from which they could make astronomical observations, to determine the correct latitude for the east-west boundary, the two surveyors selected a place near the little town of Embreeville, Pennsylvania. There they placed a large stone which is today called the Star-Gazers' Stone. From that point they began their estimates.

When they had determined the exact astronomical location of the stone, they cut a path eight or nine yards wide through the woods and brush south for fifteen miles to the point that had been decided on as the border of Pennsylvania. From there, the east-west line was run. For the next four years the party cut through the forest directly west for 233 miles. Finally they were stopped by hostile Indians, but one of the most famous boundaries in America had been drawn—the Mason-Dixon Line.

In order to mark the boundary so that it would never be disputed, the surveyors used stones brought from England, which they set at each mile. Every fifth milestone had carved on the south side the coat of arms of Lord Baltimore and on the north side that of the Penn family.

After the surveyors had completed their work and returned to England, the Royal Society asked for the astronomical records which they had made for the survey. Using these notes, the society was able to measure the exact mileage of a degree of latitude in North America. It proved to be 68.826 miles.

Two English astronomers, Charles Mason and Jeremiah Dixon, were brought from England to survey the boundaries between Maryland and the Three Lower Counties and between Maryland and Pennsylvania. Every fifth milestone had carved on the south side the coat of arms of Lord Baltimore and on the north side that of the Penns. Here, carefully preserved, is the stone that marks Delaware's southwest corner.

Many years later, when the southern states wanted to hold slaves and the northern states did not, the Mason-Dixon Line marked the division between the north and south. There are several explanations of how the southern states came to be called "Dixie," but many Delawareans claim that the nickname came from Jeremiah Dixon's last name.

Old Swedes Church

In the early days of the colony, religion and education went hand in hand. Laws as early as 1640 stated that the patrons of the colony would at all times support as many ministers and schoolmasters as the number of inhabitants seemed to require. Swedes, even if they lived far from the school or church, felt disgraced if their children could not read, and parents or an older child or neighbor taught the children between visits of the minister-teacher.

When the Dutch took over the colony, the patroons were required to furnish schoolmasters as one of the conditions for receiving grants. The first Dutch schoolmaster, Evert Pietersen, arrived with Director

93

Jacob Alrichs in the spring of 1657 and soon had twenty-six pupils. The small wooden church on the Strand at New Castle served also for the school and social club.

After the English took over the colony and new settlers began to move in from other colonies and from England, the Swedes and Dutch gradually gave up their languages for English, but they still clung to their religion. When the Reverend Eric Bjorck was sent over by the king of Sweden in 1697, he decided that the tiny log church at Crane Hook must be replaced by a new one. Although he had little money at his disposal, he persuaded the members of the congregation to begin work.

On May 28, 1698, they laid the first stones of the foundation. The Reverend Eric Bjorck said in a letter to a friend that they were laid all around about one foot deep except on the south wall and wherever a grave or some stumps interrupted. The building was thirty feet wide

The Reverend Eric Bjorck was sent from Sweden in 1697 to be pastor of Crane Hook Church near Wilmington. He decided that the most important thing to be done was to build a new church, and before the first year was over, the enthusiastic pastor succeeded in getting the first stones laid. Today Old Swedes Church, completed in 1699, is a landmark in Wilmington.

by sixty feet long. The walls were made of gray stone, three and a half feet thick to the bottom of the windows and only two feet thick from there to the roof.

A stone mason from Philadelphia with his two sons was hired to do the masonry. They charged eighty-six pounds in silver as well as sufficient meat, drink, washing, and lodging. Another Philadelphian did most of the outside carpentry, and a third did all the inside carpentry. The next year a glazier came from Holland to make the windows, and a local blacksmith made wrought-iron letters to be used for the inscriptions.

The brick floor was set on the ground and had a square of loose bricks in the main aisle, which were lifted out each year to hold the Christmas tree. The pews were made of fir, and the banisters and pulpit were carved of black walnut. It is believed that this is the oldest church pulpit in the United States.

The new church was consecrated on Trinity Sunday, June 4, 1699, and although it was named Holy Trinity Church in honor of the day on which it was dedicated, this is the church that is known as Old Swedes today.

An Artist Arrives

Eric Bjorck remained the pastor of the church he had built until the spring of 1711. At that time Andreas Hesselius was sent by King Charles XII of Sweden to relieve Bjorck. With him came his twenty-nine-year-old brother, Gustaff Hesselius, a painter.

The brothers landed first at Charleston, South Carolina, and came to Wilmington by way of the Chesapeake Bay. They had a letter of introduction from William Penn to his deputy governor, Charles Gookin, and after unpacking at Wilmington, they went to Philadelphia to present their credentials. Governor Gookin perhaps had some influence in Gustaff's getting his first commission, a portrait of the rector of Immanuel Church in Philadelphia.

Gustaff decided to live in Philadelphia, but he was constantly on the go, traveling through Delaware, Maryland, and Virginia, painting por-

Gustaff Hesselius came to Delaware with his brother, the pastor of Old Swedes Church. This self-portrait of the artist shows the expression of character for which he became famous in his portraits.

traits which were filled with character. On September 5, 1721, the first commission in America to do a painting for a public building was given to Gustaff. A Maryland church commissioned him to make a painting of "Our Blessed Savior and ye Twelve Apostles at ye last supper."

Although his work was highly thought of and well received, like most artists of his time, Gustaff Hesselius found it hard to make a living painting only portraits. On December 11, 1740, an advertisement in the *Pennsylvania Packet* stated that Gustaff Hesselius from Stockholm would do painting in the best manner of coats of arms on coaches, landscapes, signs, and showboards. He would also paint houses, ships, gild old pictures, and clean and mend them.

Gustaff also built the first organs in the colonies, one of which was for the Moravians at Bethlehem, Pennsylvania. John Hesselius, Gustaff's son, also painted portraits in Delaware and lived for a time at New Castle. John was the first teacher of the famous Charles Willson Peale of Philadelphia.

The Question of Slavery

By the time the Swedes made their first settlement on the Delaware, the slavery of African natives was an established way of life in both Europe and America. No Negroes were brought to Christina on the first boatload of colonists, but after Peter Minuit unloaded the *Grip*, he sent the ship and its crew back to the West Indies to trade. When the *Grip* returned, the skipper brought with him a Negro whom he had either captured or purchased. His name was Black Anthony, and he must have been an adaptable man. By 1648 he was the special servant to Governor Printz, and records show that in 1654 he made purchases on his own from the company that controlled New Sweden, indicating that he may have been a freeman by that time.

Black Anthony seems to have been the only representative of his race in New Sweden, but when the Dutch took over, some of the settlers brought their own slaves with them, and others imported slaves from the West Indies. Because the farms produced mostly grains, they did not require the great number of slaves that the rice and tobacco plantations of Carolina and Virginia needed.

The first census in 1677 listed 243 taxable persons under the jurisdiction of the New Castle court. Of this number, which represented probably at least a thousand total population, twelve were white servants and eight were Negro slaves. Farther up the river at Chester jurisdiction, which was settled mostly by Swedes, the census listed only one slave. From this small beginning, the Negro population grew until in 1790, when the first national census was taken, it exceeded one fifth of the total population.

Until 1700 the same laws of trial and punishment applied to Negroes as did to white servants. In 1700, however, new laws were made providing greater penalties for Negroes than for whites for certain crimes. Negroes were not allowed to carry weapons, nor could they assemble in great numbers. A special kind of trial was set up so that, instead of the usual trial by jury, Negroes were tried by two justices of the peace and six freeholders, and if they were found guilty, they were executed on the spot.

The Quakers began the first movement to free the slaves. Kent County was the first county to offer a bill to the Assembly to prohibit the importation of slaves. Members from New Castle and Sussex Counties combined to vote it down. Later, a similar bill was suggested by Dr. Charles Ridgely of Dover. It was passed by the Assembly in 1775, but was vetoed by Governor John Penn.

When the Mason-Dixon Line became the division between slave states and free, Delaware retained slavery. She served with the North during the Civil War, but when slavery was abolished, she substituted strict segregation.

The Last of the Indians

The white settlers in the Three Lower Counties had never had much trouble with the Indians. The Leni-Lenape were a friendly people, and except for the massacre of the first colony at Zwaanendael, they had offered little resistance to the intrusion of their lands. From time to time some Indian chiefs would present their grievances to the governors of the colony, but a few gifts and a new treaty satisfied them although more and more of their lands were taken over by the settlers.

After a hundred years of this pressure, the Indians of the peninsula made one final attempt to get back their lands from the white men. In 1742 Messowan, a Shawnee war chief, with twenty of his warriors arrived at a Nanticoke village on the Nanticoke River. Messowan asked Panquash, the leader of the Nanticokes, to call a meeting of all the tribes of the Indian River Indians. Panquash sent out word that there would be a meeting in the Great Pocomoke Swamp.

Indians from all parts of the peninsula came, and for six days the chiefs made speeches telling how the white men had wronged them. After the Indians had worked themselves up to a spirit of war, Messowan began to talk. He told how the Shawnees had been driven from their hunting grounds in South Carolina and Tennessee and how they

This portrait of Tishcohan, an Indian chief, was painted by Gustaff Hesselius, the first artist to come to Delaware.

had been forced to migrate to the Susquehanna Valley to live near the Iroquois-speaking Indians.

Since then, they had made friends with the French who had settled along the Mississippi River. The French had offered to help them. If the Indian River Indians would join forces with them, five hundred Shawnee warriors would come down to the Chesapeake, and together they would kill every man, woman, and child of the white people on the peninsula. Then they would go south through Virginia, killing as they went and on to South Carolina, where the Shawnee could then get back their lands. Meanwhile, the French would help the Iroquois in the north to drive out the white people who had made settlements there.

When Messowan had finished his speech, all eyes turned to an old woman, Queen Weocomocus, ruler of all the Indian River Indians. Queen Weocomocus directed her spokesman, Robin, to tell the gathering her wishes. Robin, an intelligent and active man, spoke English and acted as interpreter for meetings with the white men. Now, in a long speech, Robin told of how his people, the Assateagues, had been driven from their homes by the white settlers in Virginia and had been forced to move to the village on the Nanticoke River.

At the end of his speech, Robin said that they would ally themselves with the Shawnees to fight the white people. As soon as this agreement was reached, a ceremonial dance was begun.

The meeting had been going on for six days, and the white people in the surrounding area were well informed about it. A few soldiers were sent to the village to round up the Indian leaders. They were taken into town and imprisoned before the Shawnee allies joined them. The court records show that the Indians denied planning an attack, and since none had been made, the whites felt that to punish any of the leaders might cause more trouble.

On July 24, 1742, another treaty was signed by the Indians. They promised to go home peacefully, and the Shawnees left without incident.

The white people continued to push the Indians farther and farther back into the swamps and take their lands. A few years later the Indian River Indians took the bones of their honored dead and paddled up the Chesapeake in their log pirogues. They settled temporarily on the Susquehanna River under the protection of the Iroquois.

The Yellow People

There are no more full-blooded Indians left in Delaware, but people of mixed racial strain abound. The two chief groups of these, sometimes called collectively the Yellow People, are the Nanticokes and the Moors.

The Nanticokes or "Indians" live principally in the Indian River country of southern Delaware, the Moors principally in and near the village of Cheswold, northwest of Dover. Both have white, Indian, and Negro blood in them, and in appearance an individual Moor or Nanticoke may favor any of the three races. But they consider themselves separate from the major races and from one another. During the days of segregation, Delaware maintained schools for whites, schools for Negroes, schools for Nanticokes, and schools for Moors.

Moor and Nanticoke families have many pretty stories of how they originated. Historians think it likely that they sprang up from the intermarriage natural to a meeting between two races. Perhaps stranded pirates or shipwrecked sailors, succored by Indians or by slaves on lonely farms, were founders of these racially mixed groups. But the people themselves prefer more romantic tales of their origins.

One of the most charming is called the Egyptian legend. About 1000 B.C., the story goes, an Egyptian princess fell in love with a soldier in her father's army. Angry with his daughter, the king sent her lover on a voyage of exploration, but the princess outwitted him by going along, accompanied by a priest.

After many months of sailing, they came to an unknown land and entered a large bay, into which flowed a stream, said to have been the St. Jones. Because their ship had been battered by storms crossing the ocean, they landed and sowed grain, so that they might grow a crop while a new ship was being built to take them home again.

But when the new ship was finished, the priest, who was in league with the princess' father, seized it by force and, taking the crew, abandoned the princess and her lover to die in a wilderness far from home. The young couple survived, however, and became ancestors of the Yellow People.

This story may sound fanciful to modern ears, but it is not without some factual support. The raising of a crop of grain between two portions of a voyage was reported by Herodotus in the fifth century B.C., apparently a normal practice of seamen on long journeys. Then about a hundred years ago the rotted hull of an old ship was discovered in the mud of the St. Jones River. No pictures of it survive, but it was described as resembling a galley of ancient times far more than it did any vessel known to have visited Delaware. Also, the rare lotus lilies are said to grow only in that area, perhaps from seed carried in that long-sunk hull. And, finally, this tale was reported and published long before Thor Heyerdahl, in the voyage of *Ra II* proved that Egyptian papyrus boats could safely cross the Atlantic.

CHAPTER ELEVEN

Storm Clouds to the West

Certain colonies had no western boundaries. Their jurisdiction was regarded as extending as far west as the land went. Since no one knew just exactly how far that was, and because the range of mountains discouraged travel in that direction, for the first hundred years of settlement, little effort was made to push the boundaries of these colonies westward.

The western boundary of the Three Lower Counties was drawn at an early date. Therefore, the settlers were more interested in their own affairs than they were in what was happening west of them.

However, after England took New Netherlands from the Dutch, all the colonies from French Canada down through Carolina to Spanish Florida belonged to her. England began to look upon these widely separated colonies as one unit—the American colonies. They were rapidly becoming a large factor in English trade and would help to make her the most powerful country in Europe.

Deportation of the Acadians

There was one fly in the ointment, however. Although the Dutch had been driven out, the French were doing their best to settle the Mississippi River Valley all the way from the St. Lawrence River in Canada to New Orleans on the Gulf of Mexico. If England allowed this threat to continue, her coastal colonies would be in great danger.

Although England and France were at peace after signing the treaty of Aix-la-Chapelle in 1748, there was not room enough for both of them in America. The first activity began when it was decided that the Acadians, a small group of French Catholics whose homeland in Nova Scotia had been held by the British for many years, were a menace to the government. They were to be run out and scattered among the other English colonies where their loyalty to France would be no threat. They might have saved themselves by taking an oath of allegiance to England, but they refused to pledge themselves to fight against their own countrymen or their friends, the Indians. Ordered to leave, the Acadians begged to be allowed to join the French in Canada, but British authorities decided that they should not add their strength to the already troublesome French. They were herded into ships and dropped off a few at a time in the English colonies. This incident touched off anew the ancient enmity between England and France over their colonies in North America.

George Washington Builds a Fort

France claimed by right of discovery all the lands watered by the tributaries of the Mississippi River, but the treaty of Aix-la-Chapelle between England and France admitted England's claim as far west as the Mississippi River.

Soon after this treaty was signed, a group of London merchants and Virginia land speculators formed the Ohio Land Company. They obtained a grant of 500,000 acres of land on the east bank of the Ohio River with exclusive rights to trade with the Indians. The French immediately objected. They said that all the land drained by the Ohio River belonged to them. The English government backed the claim of the Ohio Land Company, because English settlements in the country west of the Allegheny Mountains would protect England's coastal colonies.

In 1752 the Ohio Land Company sent an agent to scout the country, make friends with the Indians, and find the easiest pass through the mountains from its storehouse at Wills Creek (now Cumberland, Maryland). The following year, learning that the French were building forts in the upper Ohio Valley, the governor of Virginia dispatched a messenger to request them to leave. The messenger's name was George Washington, and he was twenty-one years old at the time.

With a guide and four Indian interpreters, Washington reached Fort Le Boeuf about the middle of December. He delivered the governor's letter to Jacques Legardeur de St. Pierre, the French commander. The Frenchman sent a very polite letter back to the English governor telling him that, if the English wanted the French out of the Ohio Valley, they would have to send soldiers and drive them out.

When Washington returned to Williamsburg with this reply, the governor ordered him to take a company of militia, return to the Ohio territory, and drive out or kill the trespassers.

Meanwhile, a small fort which the governor had ordered built at the Forks of the Ohio had fallen to a French invasion. They rebuilt it on a larger scale and named it Fort Duquesne for their governor-general.

In late May, Washington set out with 120 men to see what could be done. About forty miles from Fort Duquesne, friendly Indian scouts told the Virginians that a French force was near. Washington hurriedly built a small stockade with a crude shelter inside, which he jokingly named Fort Necessity. Early next morning he was joined by a group of friendly Indians, and the troops started down a trail through a pile of rocks. Suddenly they came upon the French encampment, and young Washington gave the order: "Fire!"

The battle was over in fifteen minutes. Only one Virginian was killed, but ten Frenchmen were dead and twenty-two taken prisoner. In those fifteen minutes on May 28, 1754, the first blood was shed in the French and Indian War.

Washington was not so lucky the next time, however. On July 3 a French and Indian force attacked Fort Necessity, and the battle lasted nine hours. Washington surrendered, and he and the French commander worked out the terms of the treaty sitting on a log outside Fort Necessity. Washington agreed that the English would not try to build a fort west of the mountains for the next year. In exchange, he was allowed to return home with his troops.

"Join, or Die"

Before Washington reached Williamsburg, a congress was called in Albany, New York. As early as 1690, Massachusetts had tried to get the colonies to send representatives to meet and plan for their future as one unit. Most of the governors thought this was a ridiculous idea, but a few of the local leaders were beginning to favor some unified action for defense. One such man was Benjaman Franklin of Philadelphia. Weeks before the convention, he had written in the *Pennsylvania Gazette* of the dangers that would face the colonies unless they joined together to defend themselves. Beneath the article was the picture of a serpent cut into eight pieces which were named South Carolina, North Carolina, Virginia, Maryland, Pennsylvania, New Jersey, New York, and New England. Under the drawing was the caption: "Join, or Die." Because the Three Lower Counties were a part of Pennsylvania, they were not asked to send a delegate. In the local Assembly, most of the members were indifferent. Whatever Pennsylvania decided, they would abide by.

By 1754, defense was becoming a more popular topic, and Franklin took with him a plan to present to the delegates who attended the congress. Delegates came from New York, Pennsylvania, Maryland, and the New England colonies. They met with leaders of the Six Iroquois Nations to draw up a plan of defense against the encroaching French. Franklin read his plan, which called for a union of the colonies under a president appointed by the king of England. A council of delegates would be elected by the assemblies of each colony and would have legislative power subject to approval by the king and its president.

The delegates were not yet ready to act together, however. The New England authorities rejected the plan flatly, saying that it was too democratic. The union was voted down.

When the news reached England that the French were in possession of the Ohio and the American militia had been defeated, the English Parliament decided that the colonists' militia was too poorly trained and equipped to fight professional troops. In February 1755 General Edward Braddock arrived in Virginia from England with two regiments of English regulars. When Braddock learned that the American troops were composed of small, scattered bands of unorganized militia, he worked out a plan of attack on the French to try to make the best use of the available forces in America.

He did not confer with the leaders of the troops, but dealt only with the governors and delegates from each colony's Assembly. In April of 1755 at a meeting in Alexandria, Virginia, General Braddock explained to the governors of Massachusetts, New York, Maryland, North Carolina, Pennsylvania, and Virginia his plan for attacking the French. He would head an expedition to take Fort Duquesne. Governor Shirley of Massachusetts would lead his state's troops to attack Fort Niagara. William Johnson, the English Indian agent in New York, would take Crown Point on Lake Champlain.

On paper, the plan seemed workable, and all but two of the representatives from the colonial assemblies voted to support it. One representative from Georgia said that his state was so young it could spare neither men nor money. The Quaker representative from Pennsylvania said that the Friends were opposed to all war and would not take part in this one.

Although the Three Lower Counties could not send a representative to the convention, their Assembly voted to support General Braddock. They sent a herd of cattle and supplies, which included hams, cheeses, flasks of oil, raisins, spices, currants, pickles, vinegar, mustard, casks of biscuit, kegs of sturgeon and herring, chests of lemons, kegs of rum, potatoes, and tubs of butter.

Defeated by Ambush

The supplies raised by the colonies were divided between General Braddock and Governor Shirley's forces in Massachusetts. The colonies failed to raise enough money for food for the entire English forces, and General Braddock was forced to ask the home government for more.

Braddock selected George Washington to serve under him as a volunteer civilian aide in charge of the colonial forces. They had to build a road through the wilderness twelve feet wide, over which to move their wagons with the supplies and artillery. General Braddock himself rode in a coach in the usual English fashion.

Meanwhile, the French had learned that Braddock was coming, and they rallied their Indian allies and prepared to meet the English. Finally, on July 8, the troops reached the forks of the Monongahela and Turtle

106

Creek, where they had to cross the river to avoid a narrow place in the path, then cross back. As they emerged from the second ford, French and Indians rose from their ambush and began to fire.

The whooping Indians and French shot the red-coated British down row after row. They themselves remained unseen, and as this battle with an invisible enemy continued, the iron discipline of the British began to break. They fled in panic. Washington's men tried to find cover, but every tree and bush seemed to have an Indian or Frenchman behind it. Many were killed. Four bullets pierced Washington's coat, and two horses were shot from under him, but he escaped without injury. Braddock was mortally wounded, and three days later, as the army hastily retreated, he died. Washington ordered that he be buried in the middle of the road so that the footprints of the horses and men would erase any signs of his grave, and the Indians would not dig him up and scalp him. Washington read the funeral service over him.

Fortunately, the Indians did not follow them, and Washington led the beaten troops back to Williamsburg.

For five more years the war dragged on. The people in the Three Lower Counties were as well informed as any in the colonies as to what was happening. Although they held their own Assembly, they were in constant touch with Philadelphia, which had quickly grown into the largest city in the colonies. The daily traffic between Philadelphia, Wilmington, and New Castle made close communication possible. There was no newspaper in the Three Lower Counties, but everyone read the *Pennsylvania Gazette,* which was published by Benjamin Franklin.

In this way they learned that the English were driven from the Ohio region. The Earl of Loudoun was sent to the colonies as commander-in-chief of the English and American forces. He was worse than Braddock, and as more and more English troops arrived in the colonies and were quartered on the people, a resentment began to grow toward England herself.

Loudoun demanded more money and supplies from the colonies, and the Assembly at New Castle continued to raise money and supply men for the war against the French.

"George, Be a King"

When William Pitt became prime minister in England, the colonies at last had a friend. He recalled Loudoun and sent General James Abercrombie and his second-in-command, Brigadier General George Lord Howe to take Loudoun's place. When Howe asked the colonies to raise twenty thousand troops for the campaigns of 1758, they readily did so. The colonial soldiers soon realized that General Howe understood Indian fighting. Instead of the bright crimson uniforms of the British Army, he ordered that the men be dressed in leggings as a protection against thorns and insects. He ordered muskets painted black so that the sun would not reflect from them and shortened the stocks so that they could be handled more easily in the forest.

After suffering one defeat after the other, finally in November of 1758 General John Forbes, with Washington commanding a regiment of Virginia troops under his command, took Fort Duquesne. In Canada in 1759, James Wolfe sailed up the St. Lawrence River and captured Quebec. This marked the beginning of the end for the French, although the war continued in Canada until 1760. Before the news of victory reached London, King George II died at the age of seventy-six. George III became king of England and of the American Colonies.

George III, grandson of George II, was twenty-three years old when he was crowned king in 1761. George's mother, a German princess, is believed to have admonished him repeatedly, "George, be a king!" His rigid, sheltered upbringing left him ill-equipped to be a politician at a time when ideas of rights and civil liberties were undergoing great change.

CHAPTER TWELVE

The Blue Hen's Chickens

The people in the Three Lower Counties had lived a singularly free and independent life in America. Only under Swedish rule had they had a governor in direct touch with the king. Under the Dutch their governor was a deputy of the governor in New Amsterdam, and because of the slow pace of life and the great distance from there, they went about their work almost autonomously. In that respect English government under the Duke of York had been just like that of the Dutch.

When Penn took over the counties, although the seat of his government in Philadelphia was much closer, the Three Lower Counties had the audacity to demand that they have their own Assembly. Being a liberal, Penn agreed, and although their Assembly was accountable to the governor of Pennsylvania, the Lower Counties went pretty much their own way. Penn was more interested in developing Philadelphia than Wilmington or New Castle.

In the ten years preceding the outbreak of the Revolutionary War when other colonies began to grumble out loud about being mistreated by their governors or the English laws, the people of the Three Lower Counties had little to complain about. Their population was small compared with that of other colonies. Their money was made from farming rather than trade. And their small, confined borders allowed no dreams of expansion to the west.

For these very reasons, however, the little Counties knew that they were dependent on the other colonies. They read Pennsylvania newspapers and shared, as a part of that state, the growing feeling of unrest.

An Unjust Tax

The first occasion which united the colonists of the Three Lower Counties with other colonies in protesting the laws of Parliament was a call issued by the Massachusetts House of Representatives on June 8, 1765, for a congress of delegates from the colonies to meet in New York on the first Tuesday in October. Their letter stated that the congress would discuss the difficulties to which the colonies were subjected by the acts of Parliament for levying duties and taxes on the colonies—which meant the Sugar Act of 1764 and the Stamp Act of 1765. The purpose was to consider a general and united, dutiful, loyal, and humble representation of their condition to His Majesty and Parliament and to ask for relief.

The Sugar Act had long been an annoyance to American traders, although it was not rigidly enforced. In 1733 the English government had placed a heavy duty on all sugar and molasses imported into North America from the islands owned by France. This was to force the trading ships of New England particularly to purchase their sugar and molasses from the planters in the English West Indies. However, smuggling and bribery of customs officers had rendered these laws all but useless. So, in 1764, after George Grenville had become prime minister, he revised the Sugar Act, reducing duties but insisting that collection be strictly enforced.

A year later, Grenville induced Parliament to pass the Stamp Act. This law required that every marriage certificate, bill of lading, college diploma, almanac, and other official document in the English colonies must be printed on paper carrying a special government stamp. Its purpose was the raising of a revenue for defraying the expenses of defending and protecting His Majesty's dominions in America.

Most Americans believed that England's treasury had been exhausted not by defending the colonies but by wars in Europe. They also felt that they had done their share in keeping the French and Indians from overrunning their lands. Indeed, they had incurred large debts during these wars and had worked hard to pay them off. They resented being asked—required—to pay a direct tax for the chief benefit of the mother country.

When news of the Stamp Act reached America, Massachusetts was the first colony to speak against it. The other colonies were not far behind. Opposition to the measure soon appeared everywhere. The people in cities and villages gathered in excited groups and loudly expressed their indignation. Ministers denounced the scheme from their pulpits, and associations calling themselves Sons of Liberty were founded in every colony. When Massachusetts issued its call for a Stamp Act Congress, to be held in New York in October 1765, the colonies were ready for action.

Action Against the Stamp Act

This time, the Three Lower Counties were invited to send their own delegates. The Assembly had adjourned before the request was received, and since the proprietary governor in Pennsylvania was not likely to call a special session for them to vote on delegates, the Assemblymen in each county prepared a letter appointing Jacob Kollock, Caesar Rodney, and Thomas McKean as their delegates to the New York meeting. Along with their delegates, the Counties sent a written complaint of the weighty and oppressive taxes imposed on them by the acts of Parliament. They firmly asserted that the colonies had no right to be taxed without their consent.

The men chosen to represent the Three Lower Counties had been active in the politics of that area for many years. Thomas McKean was born in New London, Chester County, Pennsylvania, and was admitted to the bar in 1757, when he was twenty-three years old. He moved to New Castle County and soon became clerk of the Assembly.

Caesar Rodney, the son of William Rodney, was born in Dover, Kent County, October 7, 1728. At the age of twenty-eight he was appointed sheriff of Kent County and afterward was a judge. He represented his district in the Assembly.

Jacob Kollock was unable to attend the Stamp Act Congress in New York, so Caesar Rodney and Thomas McKean set out together. They arrived at the congress and presented their credentials, which were accepted. The first business was to elect a chairman of the congress, and the two final runners were Timothy Ruggles, a Massachusetts conservative, and James Otis, a Massachusetts radical. Although McKean and Rodney supported James Otis, the conservative Timothy Ruggles won.

Shortly before the congress, James Otis had written a pamphlet entitled "The Rights of the British Colonies Asserted." In it he borrowed an idea from a Dutch writer who had declared many years before that taxation without representation was tyranny. The pamphlet had been so well distributed and read throughout the colonies that at the congress one of the favorite phrases to be heard was "No taxation without representation!"

The members of the congress voted to oppose the Stamp Act and drew up a petition to both houses of Parliament for its repeal. Rodney and McKean supported these measures wholeheartedly, but the conservative chairman, Timothy Ruggles, refused to sign the petition. McKean later wrote to a friend that he personally pressed Ruggles so hard that Ruggles finally said it was against his conscience. McKean then called him up before the assembly to give his reasons. Next morning Ruggles left before daylight without saying good-bye to any of the other delegates.

Caesar Rodney later said to his brother that the congress was made up of people with the greatest ability he had ever seen, but that he was still awed with the thought of their petitioning the great body of Parliament.

The proceedings in New York were followed eagerly by many of the people of the Three Lower Counties. One of Rodney's cousins said that he was anxious for Rodney to return so that he could learn first-hand exactly what happened at the congress.

November 1, the day on which the act was to go into effect, was observed as a day of mourning and fasting in the colonies. Funeral processions were held in the streets, and bells tolled. The flags of sailing ships were trailed at half-mast, and newspapers outlined articles with black lines. The courts were closed, weddings were postponed, ships remained in port, and for a while all business was stopped.

Later in the day, mobs began to gather in front of the residences of officials, and the protestors burned distinguished royal figures in effigy.

112

Many of the ships loaded with stamps were boarded by Sons of Liberty, and colonial militia and the stamps were seized and burned or dumped into the water.

Some members of Parliament were alarmed by the actions of the colonists and suggested that the Stamp Act be repealed. Other Englishmen said that such a submission to insurrection in the colonies would be a disgrace to the authority of Parliament. The repeal passed, however, although the king was angry about it. He felt that compliance with the colonists' demands had weakened his power and "planted thorns under the King's pillow."

Petitions and Protests

The citizens of the Three Lower Counties were overjoyed when they learned of the repeal of the Stamp Act. A visitor to New Castle at the

Rioting broke out in all the colonies in protest against the Stamp Act.

time wrote that the little town was illuminated on the joyful occasion and really made a pretty appearance from the water.

The Assembly appointed Thomas McKean, Caesar Rodney, and George Read as a committee to write an address of thanks to the king for the repeal. George Read was born in Cecil County, Maryland, on September 7, 1733. He studied law at the Public Academy in Philadelphia (later the University of Pennsylvania) and was admitted to the bar in 1752. He served as attorney general of the Three Lower Counties from 1763 to 1774. These three men were good friends and had worked together to make the government of their counties as independent as possible from Pennsylvania. George Read was not so liberal as Rodney and McKean, but he was just as anxious to work on a larger scale to help all of the American colonies.

Hoping that things were settled, the writers loaded the address with such phrases as "the clouds are dissipated" and "Affection is unbounded for the best of Kings." It was signed "from the most loyal subjects." This document was sent through a London agent, Dennys de Berdt. De Berdt later informed the Assembly that the king was so pleased with the address that he read it twice.

In 1767, England's money problem was still unsolved. Parliament passed the Townshend Acts, laying duty on several commodities, including tea. When the Assembly of the Three Lower Counties met the following year, they unanimously approved resolutions declaring that the Townshend Acts deprived the colonists of the exclusive right of taxing themselves. A second petition to the king was framed by McKean, Read, and Rodney. It ended with the statement that although Parliament was the wisest and greatest assembly upon the earth, it was not right that people in England represent the colonies in the matter of taxation. On the same day a letter was sent to Peyton Randolph, speaker of the Virginia House of Burgesses, telling of this action.

The petitions had little effect on England, but when American Nonimportation Associations began to boycott English goods, the colonial point of view became very clear. The Three Lower Counties had no traders who imported goods directly from England. Philadelphia and

Maryland had separate nonimportation agreements, and the traders of the Three Lower Counties had an agreement with the Philadelphia association. Some of the merchants in the lower part of New Castle County complained that Maryland's agreement was less inclusive than Pennsylvania's, and they wanted to switch their trade to Maryland. The people of upper New Castle County, around Wilmington and New Castle, had agreed to support the Philadelphia agreement. During the next year the nonimportation agreement between Philadelphia and the Three Lower Counties provided that no goods were to be imported from England unless specified by the agreement and that, if anyone imported goods contrary to this pact, he would be treated as a betrayer of the civil rights of America.

In 1770 England removed all the Townshend duties except the tax on tea. Then, early in 1773, the almost bankrupt East India Company was granted a special favor. In order to restore its fortunes, it was allowed to sell its tea in America at a price lower than it sold in England. The catch was that, no matter how low the price, it included the hated tax. This tax on tea now became a major issue in the colonies. Read, Rodney, and McKean were appointed by the Assembly as a Committee of Correspondence on October 23, 1773. Their job was to keep in communication with the other colonies to find out what they were doing and what they intended to do.

The Assembly also sent a formal protest to England and warned that, if the tea were sent, both ships and cargoes might be burned. Up and down the coast, colonies received copies of one another's protests and wrote their own. Nevertheless, the tea ships arrived in American ports. Boston's Tea Party was the first to take place. The South Carolinians met the tea ship that arrived in Charleston, but rather than waste the precious cargo, they stored the tea in the basement of the Exchange and later sold it to help finance the Revolutionary War.

When news reached Philadelphia that the regular tea ship, *Polly*, had left London in September, the patriotic citizens began to make their plans to prevent her unloading. One of the first measures they took was to send a letter to the Delaware River pilots at Lewes which said:

We need not point out to you the steps you ought to take if the tea-ship falls in your way. . . . But this you may depend on, that whatever pilot brings her into the river, such pilot will be marked for his *treason* and will never afterwards meet with the least encouragement in his business. Like *Cain*, he will be hung out as a spectacle to all nations, and be forever recorded as the *damned traitorous pilot who brought up the tea ship.* . . .

signed,
The Committee for tarring and feathering

When the *Polly* came into the river early Christmas morning, the citizens held a mass meeting of eight thousand people and decided that Captain Ayres might stay one day to buy necessary supplies and to refill his water butts, but that he must then take the tea back to England.

King George's Reprisal

England did not take kindly to this treatment of her tea ships. Parliament demanded that the colonies be punished and passed the Boston Port Bill. Among other things, this bill closed the port of Boston to all traffic until the East India Company and the customs had been paid for the losses of the Boston Tea Party.

When the news of this act reached Boston by fast ship from London, the galloping couriers of Correspondence Committees spread the word southward. By the end of May Boston's plight was known to every town and village in the colonies.

General Thomas Gage, commander in chief of the army forces in North America, was ordered to go from New York to Boston. On May 13, 1774, he arrived to enforce the port bill. He blockaded the harbor with English warships, and on June 1, all shipping into and out of Boston Harbor stopped dead.

Mass meetings were held at each county seat in the Three Lower Counties. They passed resolutions calling the Boston Port Bill unconstitutional and dangerous to the liberty of the colonies. They took up a collection to be sent to the people of Boston, set up a Committee of Correspondence for each county, and asked the speaker of the Assembly to call the members together for the purpose of choosing delegates to a Continental Congress.

Caesar Rodney, the Speaker of the Assembly, was asked to call the Assembly together to elect the delegates. Only the governor had the legal right to do this, and Governor John Penn had already refused to call the Pennsylvania Assembly for the same purpose, so Rodney took matters into his own hands.

The assemblymen convened at an unofficial meeting in New Castle in August 1774. George Read, Caesar Rodney, and Thomas McKean were again elected delegates. Although they were ordered to pledge allegiance to the king, they were also told to claim for the Assembly the sole right of taxing the people of Delaware, to forbid the carrying of Americans abroad for trial, and to condemn the Boston Port Act.

Being more centrally located than New York, Philadelphia was chosen by the colonies as the meeting place for the First Continental Congress. The host city had a little trouble providing a suitable building for the group. The newly built City Tavern was too small. The State House was already fully occupied by the Provincial Assembly. Carpenter's Hall, a three-story brick structure built four years before by members of the Carpenters' Guild, was chosen. It contained a well-stocked law library, and some people thought that the selection of a guildhall would help gain support from artisans and tradesfolk who might be suspicious of the actions of lawyers and politicians.

The representatives from the Three Lower Counties were greeted by members of the Philadelphia militia as they rode into town. That night they attended a banquet given for the five hundred delegates from the colonies and the city officials. Thirty-two toasts were drunk, beginning with tributes to the king and queen and ending with a vote of confidence to John Hancock of Massachusetts, who was expected to be president of the Congress.

After seven weeks of debates from nine o'clock in the morning until three in the afternoon, the members of the First Continental Congress agreed not to import goods from or export goods to England nor to use any taxed British commodities. They recommended also that a Second Continental Congress be held in May 1775.

Read, Rodney, and McKean returned to New Castle, where they made their report to the Assembly on March 15. The Assembly promptly appointed the same three men as delegates to the Second Continental Congress.

Opening Fire

A month before the Second Continental Congress met, news came that English troops had fired on minutemen at Lexington and Concord. Emotions ran high, and the people of the Three Lower Counties were ready to fight. In every county troops volunteered, and twice a day they were drilled in military tactics. Many young Quakers enrolled, much to the horror of their elders. For this violation of their faith, they were read out of meeting.

In September of 1775, John McKinly, the president of the Council (or Committee) of Safety for the Three Lower Counties, reported that about five thousand men were ready to defend their just rights and liberties with their lives and fortunes. The river was fortified with fire rafts to attack English ships, and a spiked barricade was sunk across the channel.

The last week in March 1776, the English warship *Roebuck* entered Delaware Bay. The *Roebuck* was heavily armed and was escorted by a tender that was also armed. When he heard the news, Colonel John Haslet sent a messenger riding to Philadelphia to tell of the danger. Then he called up the militia and marched from New Castle to Lewes to protect the town. The captain of the *Roebuck* did not attack, however, but cruised up and down the coast.

One Sunday morning in April an American schooner anchored near the shore of Cape Henlopen. The captain sent word to Colonel Haslet that he needed help to unload supplies for the Americans. The American ship had been sighted by the captain of the *Roebuck*, and about the same time that Colonel Haslet and the militia started by land, the English captain sent the armed tender toward the American ship.

Between the militia and the ship was a small creek. The people who lived near the crossing brought their boats to row the men across, but the English tender was ahead of them. The American captain decided that rather than be captured by the English, he would leave. In his haste to get away he ran his ship aground, and when the militia arrived at the scene, the men on the tender were firing at the grounded ship. The soldiers fired back, but the tender was too far away for their bullets to reach it, and the balls from the English ship also fell short. The men laughed as they picked up the balls for souvenirs and began to help unload the American ship.

The tender had sent word to the *Roebuck*, and soon the big warship sailed around the cape at full speed. The captain of the American sloop turned his guns on the *Roebuck*, and she soon fled. Several Englishmen were wounded, but not a single American was hurt.

The *Roebuck* stayed in Delaware Bay, and in May she was joined by an English sloop, *Liverpool*. Together with their armed tenders the two ships sailed straight up the river toward Wilmington. The citizens of New Castle and Wilmington were thoroughly frightened. Many of them loaded what furniture and clothes they could carry into wagons and fled to the back country. At Wilmington the militia gathered together thirteen or fourteen row galleys, mounted them with guns, and stocked them with ammunition. When the English ships were sighted on the morning of May 8, crowds of people gathered on the banks to watch the battle. When the enemy ships reached the mouth of Christina Creek, the row galleys opened fire.

In the midst of the battle, an artillery major arrived on horseback. He asked a boatman to row him out to one of the galleys, but the boatman hesitated. Finally a handful of money helped him to decide to take the major out. The major took over a cannon on a galley and fired it until the ammunition ran out. When he was told there were no more balls, the frustrated major took off his boots, filled them with powder, and shot them at the enemy—a futile but splendid gesture.

The *Roebuck* tried to get closer to the galleys, but the water was so shallow at the mouth of Christina Creek that she ran aground and listed so that her guns were useless. There she stayed all night until next morning when the tide was high enough to float her off. The *Liverpool* had had enough also, and both ships sailed down to Lewes, where they stayed until the ships' carpenters could repair them.

The Delaware state bird is the gamecock, named for the mascots of Colonel Haslet's first Delaware regiment—two gamecocks, hatched from the eggs of a steel-blue hen. In numerous campfire cockfights, the cocks were never beaten, so Delawareans rushed into action shouting, "We're sons of the Blue Hen, and we're game to the end!" Residents of Delaware today still proudly call themselves the Blue Hen's Chickens.

Thus, a fleet of row galleys defeated two English men-of-war in the first naval battle of the Revolutionary War.

Sons of the Blue Hen

When Colonel Haslet's first Delaware regiment marched to Philadelphia to join Brigadier General John Cadwalader's forces, Captain Jonathan Caldwell's company from Kent County was a part of it. In their enthusiasm for action, these young men were prepared either to fight or play. They took with them two gamecocks, hatched from the eggs of a small, lean, steel-blue hen, bred in Kent County, which they insisted could outfight any other birds. In numerous cockfights lighted by campfires, the cocks were never beaten.

When the time for battle came, the men of Captain Caldwell's company rushed into action shouting, "We're sons of the Blue Hen, and we're game to the end!" They were known thereafter as the Blue Hen's Chickens, and residents of Delaware today still proudly bear this nickname.

CHAPTER THIRTEEN

The Price of Independence

In January 1776 a pamphlet urging complete independence from England appeared in the colonies. It was titled *Common Sense* and was written by Thomas Paine, an Englishman who lived in Philadelphia. The booklet became a best seller, selling 100,000 copies in less than three months. No other book in the United States has ever had such a quick, large sale relative to the population.

Newspapers in all the colonies began using the word "independence," and the Liberty Boys in the Three Lower Counties held street rallies and protests in halls, churches, or private homes, wherever they could get people to listen to their plea for separation.

Whig or Tory?

Early in June, George Read, Caesar Rodney, and Thomas McKean returned to the Continental Congress in Philadelphia. On June 7 Richard Henry Lee of Virginia introduced a resolution demanding the separation of the colonies from English rule. Several of the colonies were undecided, however. New York would lose her trade with England. In Maryland, too, many rich merchants and a few large plantation owners were content with English rule and loved their governor, Robert Eden. Most of the Quakers opposed any idea that might invite violence.

Even those who talked of instant independence were not ready to commit themselves against the moderates, who favored freedom at some later date. The delegates agreed to postpone the vote for three weeks.

George Read, one of the signers of the Declaration of Independence from Delaware, believed that too many people were unready to support rebellion and that it was too early to separate from England. Nevertheless, when Caesar Rodney and Thomas McKean voted for independence, Read gave in and made it unanimous.

It was now up to the delegates of each colonial assembly to decide how the colony would vote. Then each colony would cast one vote either for or against independence. Already, men in all the colonies were choosing sides. Many people were conservative in their thinking and wanted no change or upheaval in their way of life. They were loyal to the king and called themselves Loyalists or Tories. Other men expressed their strong feelings of liberty and patriotism to America instead of to England. They called themselves Patriots or Whigs.

George Read was a conservative and opposed independence. He firmly believed that the colonies could get along with England without being separated from her. He also understood the danger of a small, ill-equipped group of scattered colonies making war on the strongest nation in the world. He would vote against independence.

Thomas McKean was the son of Scottish-Irish immigrants, and he had worked hard to acquire his law degree. He believed fervently that independence was the only way for the colonies to get their just rights, and he supported the delegates who would vote for independence.

Caesar Rodney was an orphan who had grown up in the home of his guardian, Nicholas Ridgely. Caesar had an inheritance from his father, and Mr. Ridgely saw to it that his ward received instructions in fencing and dancing as well as in his studies. Caesar was five feet ten inches tall, had elegant manners and a good sense of humor. He had already made a place for himself in the Three Lower Counties before he began to go to Philadelphia for the meetings of the Continental Congress. He was well known and liked all over the colony and was a liberal, wanting independence for the colonies.

Soon after Lee presented his resolution to the congress, a messenger came to Philadelphia to talk with Caesar Rodney. He said that a thousand Tories had assembled in northeastern Sussex County above Lewes, on June 11. The county militia was called out to march at short notice, but members of the Council of Safety went to the Tory meeting place and talked with the leaders.

The Tories dispersed, but some of the ardent Patriots thought they should be arrested and their property confiscated. Many of the Tories continued to argue that refusing to use tea would have been enough rebellion against England without disturbing the peace and prosperity of the Counties.

The messenger told Caesar Rodney that it was important that he come to Dover and talk to the Tories. Perhaps they would listen to him and stop causing trouble. Rodney returned with the messenger and held meetings with the dissidents from Dover to Lewes, trying to make peace among them.

The Ride for Unanimity

As the time for the vote on independence drew near in Philadelphia, Thomas McKean realized that, unless Rodney returned to Philadelphia, the vote of the Three Lower Counties would become void because of a tie between himself and George Read. Read flatly refused to vote for independence, and McKean was just as stubborn in his vote for it.

Thomas McKean was an ardent supporter of independence from the beginning. When Caesar Rodney's vote was needed to pass the Declaration, McKean sent a messenger for him, and delayed the voting until he arrived. Together they persuaded George Read to vote affirmative also.

McKean knew that Rodney would vote with him, thus making an affirmative vote for the Three Lower Counties.

The debates on the Declaration of Independence had been long and arduous. There was still some opposition to voting for it at all. However, it was evident from the beginning that a majority of the colonies favored independence, but in order to make a show of solidarity it was important that the vote be unanimous. Thomas McKean had watched the proceedings very carefully, and he had been writing letters to Caesar Rodney every day, urging him to return to the congress. When news came of the arrival of a large English armament under the brothers, William and Richard Howe, at Sandy Hook, New York, immediate and united action was imperative. McKean could wait no longer. He sent a fast rider to find Caesar Rodney and tell him that he must return as quickly as possible.

Several different versions of Caesar Rodney's famous ride have been told, but one continues to persist. It says that Rodney was in love with Sarah Rowland, the daughter of the postmaster of Lewes, who was a

Tory. While Rodney was trying to quiet the Tories in that area, Sarah's father forced her to hide Thomas McKean's letters and not show them to Rodney. It was not until the messenger from McKean arrived, and a Negro maid in the Rowland house told Rodney what was going on, that he left for Philadelphia.

Whether the details of this version are true or not, the fact was that only a few hours remained between the time Rodney left the lower part of the peninsula and the time the voting took place in Philadelphia, eighty miles away. Within ten minutes after the messenger found him, Caesar Rodney was mounted and on his way to Philadelphia.

He galloped past fertile fields and across shallow creeks. When he came to an inn, he stopped only long enough to change horses. It was after dark when he passed Blackbird Forest, but on he went. At New Castle he had to take the ferry across the Christina Creek and again at Wilmington to cross the Brandywine.

Past the old blacksmith shop on Penny Hill and across the Twelve Mile Circle boundary into Pennsylvania he rode. On he went to Chester, clattering across the wooden plank bridges over the creeks on the other side.

After all night and most of the next day, the exhausted man and horse climbed slowly up the steep hill from whose top he saw the Schuylkill River. It was afternoon now, and only a few miles remained.

Meanwhile, McKean was using every tactic he knew to delay the vote. New York could not be counted on. South Carolina might go either way. Of the nine Pennsylvania delegates only three—John Morton, James Wilson, and Benjamin Franklin—were sure to vote for independence. Two were against it, and two more had refused to attend. While McKean was stalling, waiting for Rodney to arrive, Benjamin Franklin was pleading with the Pennsylvania delegates, and John Rutledge was doing his best to persuade his South Carolinians to vote "yes."

The hot muggy afternoon of July 2, 1776, dragged on. The delegates were impatient. Small black flies stung the legs of the weary delegates through their thin silk stockings. The usual dinner hour had long passed, and voices began to demand a vote. Rutledge had brought his

Caesar Rodney arrives at the State House (now Independence Hall) in Philadelphia to cast Delaware's deciding vote on the Declaration of Independence. Rodney's ride, as dramatic as Paul Revere's enabled the Declaration to be adopted unanimously.

Carolinians into line. New York decided not to vote. Franklin had persuaded his delegates who were opposed to remain silent. It looked as if the vote would be unanimous except for the Three Lower Counties.

McKean had done his best. He could not prevent the vote any longer, and the secretary rose to call the roll.

In alphabetical order, Connecticut was called first. The "yes" from that colony brought cheers from the delegation. Next came Delaware. For the first time, the colony was formally recognized as an individual colony instead of the Three Lower Counties. As Thomas McKean stood and faced John Hancock, the president, the door behind him burst open, and the exhausted Caesar Rodney stood before the congress.

The statue of Caesar Rodney making his famous ride to vote for independence. It stands in Rodney Square in Wilmington and was designed by James Kelly of New York.

When George Read saw that he was outnumbered, he agreed to vote for independence also. The vote was unanimous, and all three of the delegates from Delaware signed the Declaration of Independence two days later.

The Stars and Stripes

In September a convention of men from the Three Lower Counties met at New Castle to draw up a constitution for the State of Delaware. No longer would the Counties be mentioned in the records as the Three Lower Counties or Territories Otherwise Called Delaware. The convention members adopted a constitution and formed a government to be run by the people. This constitution was the first to be written by any state by a convention called especially for that purpose. This method has since been ratified as the only constitutional procedure for adopting or changing a state constitution. On May 12, 1777, the capital of the new State of Delaware was moved from New Castle to Dover.

More than a year before the Declaration of Independence was signed, the war had begun. George Washington was unanimously elected by the Congress to be commander in chief of the American forces on June 15, 1775, and the Battle of Bunker Hill followed two days later. The British fleet was repulsed at Hampton, Virginia, in October, and English vessels were driven from Charleston Harbor, South Carolina, in December of that year.

Before they were united, every colony had its own ensign, and during the first few months of the Revolutionary War, many different flags were flown in the battles. Several of these flags were made with thirteen red and white stripes with various insignia in the canton—the upper left-hand corner.

In December of 1775 General Washington was camped at Cambridge, Massachusetts, with his troops. They were despondent, and in order to cheer them on New Year's Eve he took from a cupboard in his headquarters a new flag with thirteen evenly spaced red and white stripes making the field and the Union Jack of Great Britain in the canton. The next morning, January 1, 1776, halyards were tied to it, and as Washington wrote, they hoisted the "Grand Union flag" in compliment to the United Colonies.

More than a year passed. General Washington had been busy and had had little time to think about the flag. A story continues to endure concerning the first flag, however, and though it is not provable, it also is not disprovable: In the summer of 1777, while George Washington was in New Jersey keeping close watch on the redcoats in New York, he, Robert Morris, and George Ross made a visit to Philadelphia to visit George Ross's niece by marriage, who was a seamstress. Betsy Griscom was a Quaker who had eloped with John Ross, an upholsterer from New Castle who was not a Quaker. The wedding resulted in Betsy's being read out of meeting. Shortly after they were married,

John Ross was killed by the explosion of some powder he was guarding on the wharves, and he left Betsy a widow at twenty-four.

Being a good seamstress, she carried on the upholstering business and was doing very well. She is believed to have supplemented her income by making ensigns and signaling flags for ships. The three callers wanted Betsy Ross to help them design a flag for the united colonies and to make it for them. Washington showed her his striped flag and asked her if the new ensign could be based on it, with white stars on a dark blue field in the canton instead of the British Union Jack. The original plan showed six-pointed stars, because the visitors had assumed that five-pointed stars were too difficult to shape. However, Betsy showed the gentlemen how to fold a piece of cloth and cut a five-pointed star with a single slash of the scissors. They evidently were impressed, because they assigned her to make the flag.

If the story is true, Betsy Ross's flag was adopted by Congress as the national flag on June 14, 1777. Less than three months later the Stars and Stripes saw its first action in Delaware.

Action at Cooch's Bridge

General Washington and Sir William Howe continued to size one another up in New Jersey and New York. On July 24, 1777, Washington learned that Howe with his well-equipped army had set sail the day before, not up the Hudson River as he had expected, but out to sea, leaving a garrison of about seven thousand to hold New York. Washington could not figure out what General Howe had in mind. Was he planning to sail up the Delaware River and take Philadelphia, because it was the seat of government of the colonies and the Continental Congress was there? Or was he heading southward to the Carolinas? Perhaps he was going to Boston instead.

Washington thought that most probably Howe was making a feint toward Philadelphia in hopes of frightening Washington into moving his army south of the Delaware River. Then Howe could quickly sail up the Hudson River, join General John Burgoyne, who was coming down from Canada, and cut the colonies in half. The Continental Congress was upset by General Howe's maneuver. They were certain that he was headed for Philadelphia. They did not want to take any chances, and sent several messages to Washington urging him to bring his army closer to Philadelphia to protect them.

On July 28 the main body of Washington's army had reached Trenton, New Jersey, on the Delaware River, and two days later he learned that Howe's fleet had been sighted off the Delaware capes. He immediately started his army toward Philadelphia, only to learn the next day that the fleet had again stood out to sea. Washington was now convinced that General Howe's maneuvering was to coax him away from New York, so he turned his army back toward Trenton, anxiously awaiting further news.

While taking care of some administrative matters in Philadelphia, General Washington was introduced to a young French nobleman, the Marquis de Lafayette, barely twenty years old, who had outfitted his own troops and ship and had come to America to help the colonies. Lafayette asked to fight with Washington. He asked no payment, say-

Monument at Cooch's Bridge commemorates the battle during which the Stars and Stripes was first flown in action.

ing that he wanted to learn, not instruct. Washington liked the young Frenchman and placed him on his staff.

On August 10, Washington received news that the English fleet had been sighted off the east coast of Maryland. He stopped his army and camped. By August 22, Washington knew that Howe planned to attack Philadelphia by way of Chesapeake Bay. He ordered the troops to march south, and next day the little American Army of about ten thousand men paraded through Philadelphia.

With his new French aide at his side, Washington rode ahead to reconnoiter. They rode through Wilmington and on to within two miles of Head of Elk in Maryland, near the headwaters of the Christina River. The English troops had begun to debark the day before. Washington and Lafayette returned to Wilmington on August 27 and joined the main army camped there.

The last of August Howe began his march toward Philadelphia through northwestern Delaware. On September 3, Washington sent General "Scotch Willie" Maxwell with about nine hundred Pennsylvania horse and seven hundred Marylanders and Blue Hen's Chickens to intercept the British under Lord Cornwallis at Cooch's Bridge, near Iron Hill in Delaware. Washington had ordered General Maxwell to fight over a wide area, forcing Cornwallis' troops to scatter out, or deploy. Ahead of General Maxwell and his troops as they marched toward Cooch's Bridge was the new flag of Stars and Stripes, unfurled for the first time in a battle.

The American troops were ill equipped and heavily outnumbered. But they fought stubbornly until their general thought he had accomplished his mission and ordered them to withdraw. Thirty Americans were wounded and killed in this, the only battle of the Revolution fought on Delaware soil.

The nearby home of Thomas Cooch, who was a colonel in the Revolutionary Army, was taken over by Lord Cornwallis for his headquarters. The house is still occupied by the Cooch family today.

A Defeat on the Brandywine

General Howe and his thirteen thousand troops continued to advance very slowly. After six weeks cooped up on shipboard, the men needed time to regain their land legs and to absorb some of the fresh meat which they took from the well-stocked Delaware farms. Howe also needed to replace some of his cavalry and draft horses which had died during the voyage. By September 19 the English Army reached Kennett Square, Pennsylvania, and Howe felt that he was ready for action.

Meanwhile, Washington and Lafayette had carefully scouted the countryside around Wilmington to find the most advantageous site for a defensive battle. They selected the banks of the Brandywine River a few miles north of the Delaware-Pennsylvania boundary at Chadd's Ford, Pennsylvania, believing that Howe would try to cross the Brandywine there.

General Howe, with Cornwallis and several Tory guides, scouted the countryside west of the Brandywine. The English general also received information of Washington's position on the east bank from Tory spies. He decided that instead of crossing at Chadd's Ford as Washington evidently expected, he would let a small force engage the Americans' attention there. Meanwhile, Cornwallis would move north and cross the Brandywine farther up the river, then come around the American right flank and cut them off from retreat to Philadelphia.

Cornwallis began moving his eight thousand men at dawn on September 11. During the morning Washington received word of this movement from a scout, but later in the day he heard from another that no British troops had been seen around the upper fords. At one fifteen another messenger brought word that the English were about a half mile north of Birmingham Meeting House. By four o'clock Washington heard sounds of heavy cannonading from the right. He knew then that the English had managed to cross the river and were attacking him. With a local guide, General Washington and General Nathanael Greene retreated with Greene's two brigades following. About dark, General Anthony Wayne and General Maxwell withdrew their infantry in good order, and the Battle of the Brandywine was ended.

An amateur army and an amateur general had been defeated by professionals. The Americans were cheerful, however, as they marched

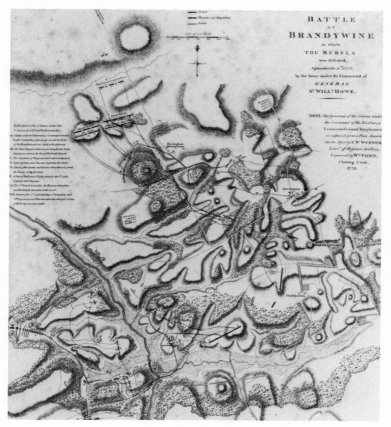

In September 1777, Washington sent General "Scotch Willie" Maxwell with
some Blue Hen's Chickens to slow up the British under Lord Cornwallis at
Cooch's Bridge in Delaware. The English troops forced the Americans to retreat,
and at the subsequent Battle of the Brandywine they gave Washington one of
his worst defeats.

from Chester toward Germantown, Pennsylvania. They believed that
they had inflicted more casualties than they had received, and their
faith in General Washington was stronger than ever.

Washington realized that unless he retreated beyond Philadelphia, he
could be penned up. As he withdrew from the city, the Continental
Congress moved to Lancaster and after that to York.

That winter, in order to keep an eye on General Howe in Philadelphia, Washington went into winter quarters with his army at Valley Forge, an easily defensible site in the hills along the Schuylkill.

The "Belle of Delaware"

No one knows why a soldier is more glamorous to a woman than other men. History is filled with such stories, and one of the most romantic is that of Mary Vining, who was often called the Belle of Delaware.

Mary was the daughter of Chief Justice Vining. She and her brother lived in a beautiful house in Dover facing the town square. Mrs. Vining died when the children were quite young, and when Mary was only fourteen, their father died also. He left a large fortune to be divided between the brother and sister, so that Mary was one of the wealthiest young ladies in Delaware.

Mary spent a good part of her time in Philadelphia, where she attended school and had her dresses made in the latest style. By 1777, when General William Howe captured Philadelphia, Mary Vining was one

Mary Vining, 'the Belle of Delaware,' was one of the most beautiful and wealthy young ladies of the Revolutionary period. This illustration is a copy of a miniature painted by Major John André.

of the most beautiful and popular young ladies in the city, and both English and American officers courted her. Many of her friends wondered why Mary did not get married, but she said very frankly that she had become so accustomed to the attention of many men that she could not be content with one.

However, as the war went on, Mary began to hear many stories about one American man—"Mad Anthony" Wayne. Some said he was vain, arrogant, and selfish. Others praised him as the most brave and brilliant of General Washington's officers. When Mary Vining met Anthony Wayne, she knew that he was the one man she could love. Her friends could not understand her infatuation. Although General Wayne was brave, honest, and generous, he was a countryman, who had been reared on a farm and had none of the polished manners of some of the other officers who were in love with her. Besides, he was married.

Mary refused to consider anyone else, and when the war ended, she was almost forty years old. But the pair still could not marry, for Mrs. Wayne was still alive.

The general spent some years in the South. Then in 1792, Washington, then President, had a new assignment for him. He was to train a force of soldiers and subdue the Ohio Indians, who had twice defeated American expeditions sent against them. In August 1794, near what is now Maumee, Ohio, he won the Battle of Fallen Timbers.

That same year his wife died, and when he came home from the frontier on leave, he asked Mary Vining to marry him. She accepted, and they planned to have their wedding the following January. Anthony gave her a set of Lowestoft china, and Mary refurbished her house from top to bottom.

In December that year, Wayne had to go west again to make a treaty with the Indians. He promised to be back in time for the wedding, but on New Year's Day a messenger brought word to Mary Vining that the brave general had died at Presque Isle on Lake Erie and been buried there.

Mary packed away her wedding dress and all the other beautiful clothes she had in her trousseau. She put on black mourning and refused to wear anything else the rest of her life.

A short while later, Mary's brother died, and she discovered that he had spent all of her inheritance as well as his own. She was no longer wealthy. The only thing she owned was a small house called The Willows in Wilmington, which had once belonged to her mother.

She sold all of her possessions—her carriages, horses, and furniture. She dismissed all but one servant and moved into the little house. The one thing she kept from her wealthy life was the set of china from General Wayne, which is still preserved and can be seen in the Ridgely house in Dover.

Her brother had left four children, and Mary spent the rest of her life helping take care of them and seeing that they received a good education.

CHAPTER FOURTEEN

Internal Strife

As the war continued, the lines between the Tories and the Whigs grew more distinct. Those opposed to independence were Tories, and those in favor of it were Whigs.

In Delaware many of the Whigs treated the Tories as enemies, calling them traitors. One patriotic Whig described a Tory as "a person whose head was in England, whose body was in America and whose neck ought to be stretched."

New Castle County was the strongest of the three counties for independence, and when a minister spoke out there against the rebels, he was converted to the Whig cause by being tarred and feathered.

An anonymous letter in the *Pennsylvania Ledger* stated that the citizens of Kent County still loved King George. And, the writer said, if the king's flag were raised, nine out of ten persons would join it. The Dover Sons of Liberty were outraged and set out to find the man who had written the letter. They discovered that Robert Holliday, a Quaker, was the author, and they demanded that he write a retraction.

John Cowgill of Duck Creek, another Quaker, refused to accept Continental paper money on religious grounds. He was denounced as an enemy to the country. Millers refused to grind his corn, and the schoolmaster sent his children home.

The Problems of Statehood

Many residents of Sussex County were still faithful to England. One Tory who had been run out of Maryland found friends in lower Delaware. He wrote to an English officer that he knew three men who would rather enlist in the English army than fight with the traitors. Enoch Anderson left Dover to go to Lewes with a company of three hundred militia, and on the way he was surrounded by about fifteen hundred Tories who called him the "d——d Patriot." Anderson quickly sent word to Thomas McKean at New Castle, and McKean sent the Kent County militia as reinforcements. On the way, the militia heard that the Tories had disbanded, so they turned around and went back. The next day the Tories began to gather again. This time Caesar Rodney asked the Assembly to send a thousand men. Upon their arrival at Dover, the Tories fled, but the militia rounded up the leaders and forced them to swear allegiance to the Assembly and the State of Delaware or be jailed.

Although Caesar Rodney had been instrumental in having the Declaration of Independence accepted, he did not have as much power in the new State of Delaware as did the conservative George Read. When the Assembly met in July, it approved the Declaration of Independence and directed each county to elect ten delegates for a constitutional convention. Whigs and Tories set out to elect their candidates. In Kent County the top Whig candidate received 150 votes less than the lowest Tory victor. New Castle, the most liberal county, chose both Whigs and Tories. With the backing of the conservative George Read, the Tories were seated in Sussex County. The Whigs were bitterly disappointed, and Caesar Rodney wrote in a letter of the "folly and ingratitude of the people."

The conservative convention set up a conservative constitution with a government almost like the one they had under the English rule. Everyone thought that the Tories in Sussex County would be satisfied, but when the time came to elect the members of the new Assembly, the Tories turned out en masse. Henry Fisher later wrote that they demanded an ax from him to chop down the Liberty Pole. When he refused, they threatened to "roast him alive."

When the Continental Congress in Philadelphia heard about the Tories, it sent part of a Virginia regiment to Dover to be sure that no violence broke out. George Read immediately complained that the Congress was invading Delaware's state rights because the Assembly had not asked for the troops.

The elections in the two lower counties turned out to be similar to that in Sussex. George Read seemed to have control of the entire state, and the Tories elected their candidates in both Kent and New Castle Counties.

Delegates to the Continental Congress were elected at once. George Read was reelected, but Caesar Rodney and Thomas McKean were replaced by John Dickinson and John Evans of Newark, both conservatives. In February 1777 the assembly chose the first president for the State of Delaware. John McKinly, a Wilmington physician and militia officer, who was said to be a lackey for George Read, was elected. His Tory views made him acceptable to the Kent and Sussex conservatives while his Scotch-Irish Presbyterianism helped him in New Castle County.

President McKinly's administration was brief, however. When the British Army landed at Head of Elk in September of 1777 and started toward Philadelphia, General Howe sent a detachment to Wilmington, which captured the president along with many of the public records and accounts. The captured president was reported to be lodged in Philadelphia with some of his Tory friends and seemed to be very happy.

The state constitution provided that, in the event of the president's death, inability, or absence from the state, the president of the Legislative Council would preside. George Read held this position, but he was with the Continental Congress which had been forced to flee Philadelphia when that city was taken by General Howe. The British occupied both Wilmington and Philadelphia, so until Read could make the hazardous journey through New Jersey and across the Delaware River without being recognized, Thomas McKean, who was speaker of the lower chamber of the Assembly, acted as president of Delaware. Striving to make the most of his position to encourage the Whigs, he was constantly hunted by the English. To add to his troubles, the State of Delaware had not a shilling in the treasury.

The elections in 1777 were no better. The Tories had grown more conservative, and the Whigs were thought to be radicals. The Whigs, however, were gaining strength, and when the Assembly met in March 1778 to elect a new president, George Read asked to be relieved of his duties, and President McKinly was still being held by the British. Caesar Rodney was elected the second president of Delaware by a vote of 20 to 4.

Tories were appointed to all the judgeships in the state by the Loyalist officials who still held power, with the understandable thought that a Tory judge would not punish a Tory offender.

Aiding the Enemy

A certain man was accused of selling poultry to the English seamen on board the *Roebuck* in New Castle Harbor. Although the evidence against him was ample, the judge freed him. When four Delaware Tories were captured and jailed in Pennsylvania, the Assembly demanded that they be returned to Delaware by state rights. Pennsylvania agreed, but when they were returned home, they received no punishment in Delaware. The Sussex County treasurer, a Tory, embezzled £387 from the county treasury, but no attempt was made to arrest him until after he had left the county.

As more and more of these crimes went without being punished, the people began to criticize the Tory leaders for the poor government. This public opinion finally forced the Assembly to pass the first act against the Tories. It was entitled An Act to Punish Treason and Disaffected Persons, and for the Security of the Government. The law stated that anyone who aided the enemies of the state should be punished.

On the oaths of two witnesses, a person could be convicted of making war against the state or aiding the king's cause. Such traitors should be put to death without benefit of clergy, and their lands should be confiscated except for the dowry of the widow. Anyone who preached or wrote in behalf of the king should be fined. This last provision made things difficult for the ministers of the Episcopal Church, the Church of England. The new law appeased the Whigs somewhat, but the Tories still remained active.

Although the Patriots had done their best early in the war to keep the king's ships out of the river, when General Howe took Philadelphia and occupied Wilmington, a number of British men-of-war were anchored off the coast of Delaware. The soldiers and sailors aboard these ships demanded supplies from the citizens, and the Tory sympathizers were only too glad to sell them beef, poultry, vegetables, and grain.

The patriotic citizens of Sussex County were disgusted. They said that the Tories and redcoats fished and shot game together along the shore and that the sheriff was purchasing cattle for the British.

Caesar Rodney, now a brigadier general, had been rounding up Tories for several months along the Mispillion, Duck, and Murderkill Creeks where he captured two men who had been selling cattle to the English. With two hundred Delaware militia, Rodney went to Sussex County to go Tory-catching. He rounded up twenty or thirty Tories in the upper part of the county who were trading with the English and took them to the Dover jail along with their two cartloads of sheep, poultry, and fruit. That night a mob of outraged Sussex County Tories threatened to march against Dover. About ten of them were imprisoned. The British threatened to take vengeance on the town for confining their friends in prison, which left Chief Justice William Killen in a dilemma. He did not dare release the prisoners, because Rodney and the militia were in the area, but he also feared the troops from the English ships. Fortunately, they did not carry out the threat.

When General Sir William Howe sailed his fleet into the mouth of the Delaware River on his way to Head of Elk, several pilots from Lewes joined it. One man on board the ships tried to persuade Howe to land there, telling him that he could easily recruit six thousand Delawareans who would march with him on Philadelphia. Howe seriously considered landing at New Castle or Wilmington instead of Head of Elk, but he was afraid that Washington might be able to move his army into either Wilmington or New Castle before he could get there, so he selected the Chesapeake instead.

So long as the British Army remained in Philadelphia, the Tories felt that they still had control of Delaware. But after Philadelphia was evacuated in June 1778, the Tories in Delaware did not feel so secure. Caesar Rodney was president from 1778 to 1781, and by that time the Whigs had managed either to drive out or to put down most of the Tories in the state.

The Black Camp Rebellion

The Tories made one last stand in August 1780. President Rodney learned that a band of several hundred Tories were again harassing the citizens of Sussex County. Rodney sent a man to investigate. He discovered about four hundred Tories meeting at Black Camp, where they were instructed and drilled by one Battholomew Banum. They planned to take all arms from the citizens in the county and kidnap the officers of the militia.

General Rodney and the militia surprised the Tories and captured many of them. Thirty-seven were indicted by the Supreme Court of Delaware in October 1780. The ringleader, Battholomew Banum, managed to escape, however, and the Assembly offered a reward for him.

A ghastly sentence was passed on the captured Tories. They were ordered to be hanged by the neck; then their heads must be severed from their bodies, and their bodies cut into four quarters—the standard English sentence for treason. Apparently, however, all the Tories were later pardoned by the lenient Assembly.

CHAPTER FIFTEEN

Peace and Amnesty

While the Tories and Whigs fought one another in Delaware, General Washington and the American forces were fighting in all thirteen colonies. In 1776 Colonel John Haslet's regiment of Delaware militia joined the Continental troops in Philadelphia. A young man, only twenty-two, named Peter Jaquett was a member of the regiment, and on the night of October 22, along with some Virginia and Maryland units, they made a surprise attack on the English at Mamaroneck, New York, but they were repulsed. On the day of the battle of White Plains, General Washington sent Colonel Haslet and the Delaware Regiment to reinforce Chatterton's Hill, and when the Hessians and British advanced on the hill, Peter Jaquett and his company slowly and deliberately withdrew, covering the retreat of the Continental troops. Jaquett fought again at Cooch's Bridge in September of 1777 and went on to the Battle of the Brandywine a few days later.

In May of 1778, Sir William Howe was replaced by Sir Henry Clinton, who turned his attention to the south. The British Army in Philadelphia evacuated that city in June and moved across the river to New Jersey.

June of 1778 found Peter Jaquett and the Blue Hen's Chickens with General Washington at the Battle of Monmouth in New Jersey. The Delawareans aided General Greene in holding the British Army and proved that they were a match for the redcoats.

On December 29, 1778, the British troops captured Savannah, Georgia, and a year later, General Clinton sailed from New York to attack Charleston, South Carolina.

Delawareans Fight in the South

George Washington's army in the north was not as large as he needed there, but he knew that General Benjamin Lincoln could not hold Charleston against Clinton. He hurriedly sent a division of Maryland and Delaware Continentals under the command of Major General Johann de Kalb to help Lincoln. Peter Jaquett, now a captain, and his troops had only gotten as far as southern Virginia when they heard that Charleston had fallen.

General de Kalb and his troops joined General Horatio Gates, who had just been appointed commander of the Southern Department. De Kalb did not approve of Gates's plans, but he and about six hundred of the Maryland-Delaware brigade, including Captain Jaquett and his company, accompanied Gates to Camden, where they encountered the British on August 16, 1780. Although De Kalb and his men fought bravely, General Cornwallis and Colonel Banastre Tarleton were too much for them. De Kalb was killed, and many of his men were killed or taken prisoner. Gates deserted his army and fled to Charlotte, North Carolina. Captain Jaquett and the three hundred Maryland and Delaware Continentals who were still alive followed slowly.

Brigadier General Daniel Morgan had been in retirement because of his severe arthritis, but when he heard of Gates's defeat at Camden, he lost no time riding to Charlotte to offer his services. On October 14, General Nathanael Greene was appointed to take General Gates's place as commander of the southern army. He arrived in Charlotte on December 4.

General Greene soon showed both the men under him and General Cornwallis that he was a better general than Gates. He sent Morgan with Captain Jaquett's Delaware Continentals, about two hundred Virginia veterans, and eighty Continental dragoons, toward the Catawba River. Cornwallis sent Tarleton to attack Morgan, and on January 17, 1781, they met at a clearing just south of the North Carolina–South Carolina border called the Cowpens. When Morgan ordered the little army into place, Captain Peter Jaquett and his company were between the Virginia riflemen and the Georgia militia. Morgan limped from campfire to campfire, encouraging the men and telling them how, when they returned home, the girls would kiss them for their gallant conduct.

When Tarleton attacked, Captain Jaquett's company pretended to retreat, catching the British between the two flanks of the American forces. After a short battle, Tarleton and the few men not taken prisoner turned and galloped off the field.

In March, Captain Robert Kirkwood with his elite Delaware company of Continental light infantry arrived to join General Greene. Captain Jaquett had been made a major, and he and his troops welcomed the Delawareans heartily and asked for news from home. A few days later they fought with Virginians and Marylanders at the Battle of Guilford Courthouse in North Carolina. For more than two hours they held their ground, until Cornwallis ordered his three artillery pieces to fire grapeshot into both his own men and the Delaware regiment. Major Jaquett and Captain Kirkwood withdrew along with the other Continentals.

At Hobkirk's Hill, overlooking Camden, South Carolina, on April 25 while Greene's troops were drawing rations, Lord Rawdon, a young British commander only twenty-six years old, attacked unexpectedly. Major Jaquett and Captain Kirkwood immediately led their forces to the bottom of the hill to delay the English while Greene formed his army above. When Greene had organized his men, the Delawareans fell back to join the other force. When the Maryland troops panicked, the Delaware and Virginia troops held the line, but General Greene ordered a retreat. Kirkwood and Jaquett, holding the British dragoons at bay, rescued all of the American wounded on the battlefield before they joined their commander.

Throughout the summer of 1781 Major Jaquett and the Delaware troops stayed in South Carolina, and in September they met the British at Eutaw Springs. When the Americans pushed the enemy beyond their camp, the Continentals could not resist the temptation to loot. Suddenly, the troops were completely disorganized, and General Greene, realizing what had happened to his army, ordered Kirkwood, Jaquett, and Lee to fall back. The next morning the English deserted the field and returned to Charleston.

Major Jaquett, Captain Kirkwood, and the Delaware troops had helped General Greene win a hard-fought campaign without having been able to gain a single tactical victory.

A Waving, Shouting General

By June 1, 1781, General Cornwallis and Colonel Tarleton had both moved into Virginia. General Lafayette had been sent by Washington to try to capture Benedict Arnold, who was making raids for the British Army in that state. Then French squadron under the command of the Comte de Barras was blockaded at Newport, Rhode Island, and was helpless. Jean Baptiste de Vimeur, Comte de Rochambeau, who was the head of the French forces in America, sent word to Washington, who was camped at Dobbs Ferry, New York, that Admiral Comte François Joseph Paul de Grasse, with a large French fleet had finally been able to break through the British blockade and was in the West Indies headed for America.

Rochambeau wanted to use the French fleet and his French Army in Virginia against Cornwallis, but Washington preferred to attack New York. Then, on August 15 Washington received a letter from de Grasse which said that the French fleet would leave the West Indies for Chesapeake Bay on August 13 with three thousand troops from Haiti. He decided to take Rochambeau's advice and attack Cornwallis in Virginia.

Leaving a garrison at West Point, General Washington started out ahead of the French Army. Eight days later the Americans were opposite the lower end of Manhattan Island. Washington hoped that General Clinton was fooled into thinking that he was planning to attack New York. Not only was Clinton fooled, but most of Washington's troops were also in the dark as to where they were going.

Washington had planned to transport the two armies on boats along inland waterways. From Trenton they would sail down the Delaware to Wilmington, from which a twelve-mile march would take them to the northern tip of Chesapeake Bay at the Head of Elk, where the British under General William Howe had disembarked four years before.

146

On his arrival at Trenton he had expected to find a fleet of small boats waiting to take the troops southward. The British had destroyed much of the shipping in the Delaware River when they occupied Philadelphia, however, and hardly enough boats were available to carry the heavy baggage.

When the American soldiers were ordered to cross the Delaware River, the New England and New York troops realized that they were being carried far from home. They threatened to desert, and Washington feared that they would mutiny unless he could give them some encouragement. He galloped to Philadelphia to beg the governor, congressmen, and businessmen to give him food, clothing, and equipment. In particular, he bombarded Robert Morris, the Superintendent of Finance, with pleas for specie enough to give the troops a month's pay in what they had not seen for years: hard money. Morris replied that he was rounding up all the gold he could find but for Washington not to be too optimistic.

Morris underrated his own abilities as a finance minister and the power of his personal business credit. For Morris was considered by everyone, at home and abroad, a far better financial risk than the country he represented. He hastily called on every source of money that he knew —requisitions on individual states, loans from the French, money borrowed on his personal guarantee of repayment, outright advances from his own pocket—and he came up with the amount General Washington needed. The men were paid, and the army advanced toward Yorktown.

Washington remained in Philadelphia until Rochambeau and the armies caught up with him. Then, leaving the French general in command in Philadelphia, Washington rode ahead toward the Head of Elk, down the same road he had taken before in an effort to head off the English landing.

Rochambeau with his staff commandeered a small boat and started down the Delaware River. It was September 5, 1781, when the little boat approached the waterfront at Chester. One of Rochambeau's officers said later that they saw an amazing sight. A tall officer in blue and buff regimentals was jumping up and down, waving his hat in one hand

and a white handkerchief in the other, to attract their attention. The dancing figure looked like His Excellency, General Washington, but that, of course, was impossible!

The boat came closer. The figure was indeed General Washington, and not only was he jumping and waving but shouting. They heard the word "de Grasse." Admiral de Grasse and his fleet had been sighted at the mouth of Chesapeake Bay.

Upon returning to Head of Elk with the army, Washington spent the next three days searching for boats to help transport his army. When the troops were all loaded, the commander in chief of the American Army rode out of Maryland toward Mount Vernon. He had not been home for seven years.

Surrender and Reconciliation

After twenty days of siege, Cornwallis surrendered at Yorktown on October 19, 1781. However, the war was not over for Major Peter Jaquett and the Delaware troops. They remained in the south, to help drive out the British there. At last, on November 16, 1782, they left their camp on the Ashley River in South Carolina to march home. Through Camden, South Carolina, to Petersburg, Virginia, they trudged, and on January 12 they arrived at Georgetown, Maryland. Five days later they crossed Christina Bridge, having marched more than five

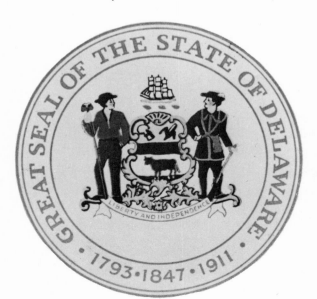

The legislature first adopted the design for the Great Seal of the State of Delaware on January 17, 1777. The *Kalmar Nyckel*, the Swedish ship which brought the first permanent settlers, is shown at the top. The cow, sheaf of wheat, ear of corn, and hoe denote the state's agriculture. The man at the right with the rifle symbolizes participation in the Revolution.

thousand miles from the time they started south, April 13, 1780, until they returned home in 1783.

Deleware furnished more troops for the Revolutionary War in proportion to its population than any other colony. The two regiments which fought in the South were reduced to a corporal's guard by the time they returned home.

Major Peter Jaquett married Eliza Price of Chester, Pennsylvania, and lived to be eighty years old. He is buried in the graveyard at Old Swedes Church in Wilmington.

Though the war had ended, the problem of what to do with exiled Tories who wanted to return to their former homes had to be solved. The Whigs did not intend to share their hard-earned victory with those they considered traitors. When one former Loyalist returned to Wilmington from New York in 1783, the magistrate ordered him to leave the state by nine o'clock the next morning.

The members of the Delaware Regiment resolved that they would not allow refugees from Delaware or any other of the United States to live within the district of this regiment, and if they discovered any, they would be punished worse than robbers or common murderers. Not until 1789 did the Assembly decide to grant the Tories amnesty and allow them full citizenship.

The Acorn Becomes an Oak Tree

When the war was over, the citizens of Delaware settled down to a happy and peaceful way of life. They did not seem to mind that Philadelphia continued to grow faster than Wilmington. They could not foresee that, twenty-five years later, a Frenchman, Éleuthère Irénée Du Pont, fleeing from another revolution, would choose the Brandywine as the location for his black-powder mills—foundation stone for a vast industrial empire that would one day make little Delaware one of the wealthiest and most powerful regions in the world.

On December 7, 1787, Delaware ratified the Constitution of the United States, the first of the thirteen former colonies to do so. Thus the little colony founded by Swedes, nourished by Dutch, and exploited by Quakers qualified for the title of First State of the Union.

Bibliography

Acrelius, Israel, *A History of New Sweden, or The Settlements on the River Delaware*, trans. by William M. Reynolds. Philadelphia: The Historical Society of Pennsylvania, 1874.

Bailey, Bernardine Freeman, *Picture Book of Delaware*. Chicago: Whitman, 1960.

Bevan, Wilson Lloyd, ed., *History of Delaware, Past and Present*. 4 vols. New York: Lewis Historical Publishing Company, Inc., 1929.

Bleeker, Sonia, *The Delaware Indians, Eastern Fishermen and Farmers*. New York: William Morrow and Son, Inc., 1953.

Canby, Henry Seidel, *The Brandywine*. New York: Farrar and Rinehart, 1941.

Carpenter, Allan, *Delaware*. Chicago: Children's Press, 1967.

Clay, Jehu Curtis, *Annals of the Swedes on the Delaware*. Chicago: The Swedish Historical Society of America, 1914.

Delaware: A Guide to the First State. American Guide Series. New York: Hastings House, 1938.

Ferris, Benjamin, *A History of the Original Settlements on the Delaware*. Wilmington, Del.: Wilson and Heald, 1846.

Macdonald, Betty Harrington, *Historic Landmarks of Delaware and the Eastern Shore*, ed. by Jeannette Eckman. Wilmington, Del.: Delaware State Society, Daughters of the American Colonies, 1963.

Pyle, Katherine, *Once upon a Time in Delaware*, Emily P. Bissell, ed. New York: E. P. Dutton and Company, n.d.

Reed, H. Clay, *Delaware, a History of the First State*. New York: Lewis Historical Publishing Company, Inc., 1947.

Scharf, J. Thomas, *History of Delaware, 1609–1888*. 2 vols. Philadelphia: L. J. Richards and Company, 1888.

Taylor, Alice, *Maryland and Delaware*. Garden City, N.Y.: Nelson Doubleday, Inc., 1964.

Weslager, Clinton A. *Delaware's Forgotten Folk: The Story of the Moors and Nanticokes*. Philadelphia: University of Pennsylvania Press, 1943.

Wildes, Harry Emerson, *The Delaware*. New York: Farrar and Rinehart, 1940.

Important Dates

1609   August 28. Henry Hudson, exploring for the Dutch East India Company, discovers Delaware Bay and River.

1613   August 27. Captain Samuel Argall names present-day Cape Henlopen Cape De La Warr, for Sir Thomas West, third Baron De La Warr, governor of Virginia.

1615   Captain Cornelius Hendricksen finds three white men near the site of Wilmington. They were the first white men known to have walked on Delaware soil.

1631   April. Zwaanendael settled by Dutch patroons with twenty-eight colonists, who were later massacred.

1632   December 6. David Peterson De Vries arrives at Zwaanendael and finds the colony wiped out.

1638   March 29 (or earlier), Peter Minuit arrives at The Rocks near present-day Wilmington to found the first Swedish settlement in Delaware.

1640   April 17. Reorus Torkillus, first Lutheran minister to have a charge in this country, arrives at Fort Christina.

1643   February 15. Governor Johan Printz arrives at Fort Christina in New Sweden.

1651   July–August. The Dutch director of New Netherlands, Peter Stuyvesant, builds Fort Casimir at what is now New Castle.

1654   May 21. Johan Classon Rising, the new Swedish governor, captures Fort Casimir and names it Fort Trinity.

1655   Peter Stuyvesant recaptures Fort Trinity and renames it Fort Casimir. September 15. Fort Christina surrenders to the Dutch. November 29. Jean Paul Jaquet appointed governor for the Swedish colony.

1657   April 21. Jacob Alrichs arrives as vice-director. Names the town near Fort Casimir New Amstel. December 30. Jacob Alrichs dies. Alexander D'Hinoyossa becomes director.

1664   October. Sir Robert Carr takes the Three Lower Counties for the Duke of York.

1673   Dutch retake the colony on the Delaware river.

1674 All Dutch possessions in North America returned to England by the Treaty of Westminster.

1682 October 28. William Penn, new Quaker proprietor, arrives at New Castle and becomes governor of the Three Lower Counties.

1698 Pirates pillage the town of Lewes.

1699 June 4. The Swedish church at Christina is dedicated.

1700 Captain Kidd visits Delaware Bay, and Lewes residents trade with him.

1701 Twelve Mile Circle is established with New Castle as center.

1711 Gustaff Hesselius, first notable painter in America, arrives in Wilmington.

1717 Commissioners appointed to lay out town of Dover as county seat of Kent.

1730 First streets of Willingtown surveyed by orders of Andrew Justison, father-in-law of Thomas Willing.

1735 William Shipley buys land in Willingtown after his wife, Elizabeth, discovers it from a dream.

1742 Last effort by Indians to regain lands.

1763 Charles Mason and Jeremiah Dixon brought from England to survey boundaries between Pennsylvania and Maryland.

1774 August 22. Caesar Rodney, Thomas McKean, and George Read appointed as delegates to the First Continental Congress.

1776 May 8. The *Roebuck* and *Liverpool* defeated by a fleet of row galleys at the mouth of Christina Creek in the first naval battle of the Revolution.

July 1–2. Caesar Rodney makes his famous ride from Dover (or Lewes) to Philadelphia to break the tie between Read and McKean, making Delaware's vote for independence affirmative.

September. Convention called at New Castle especially for the purpose of framing the first constitution for Delaware. Delaware was the first state to use this procedure, which was later ratified as the only acceptable way of framing or changing a state constitution.

1777 September 3. Battle of Cooch's Bridge, only Revolutionary War engagement on Delaware soil and the first action in which the Stars and Stripes was unfurled.

1783 Major Peter Jaquett and the few remaining troops of the Delaware Regiment return home after having marched more than five thousand miles to help fight the war in the South.

Historic Sights

Dover

The *Green* was laid out in 1717 according to William Penn's order of 1683. Here the First Delaware Regiment was mustered and marched away to join Washington's army.

Ridgely House, the home first of Thomas Parke, was built in 1728, which date is carved on a rafter beneath the roof. As a child, Mary Vining often visited here, and displayed in the house is the Lowestoft china set given to her by General Anthony Wayne, who died before they could be married.

The *Loockerman House* was built in 1742 by Vincent Loockerman, a descendant of Govert Loockerman, who came to Delaware from Holland. Vincent Loockerman was an ardent Whig during the Revolution, but among the glassware collection are two pre-Revolutionary goblets, one inscribed, "A toast to the King of England" and the other "Drink to His Majesty's Fleet."

Christ Church was built in 1734 with a floor of brick laid in the ground and a gallery for slaves.

Lewes

Zwaanendael House is a smaller-scale adaptation of part of the Town Hall at Hoorn, Holland, the home of Captain David Pietersen De Vries, who sent the first settlers to Delaware. It was built in 1931 by the state as a tercentenary memorial and has a statue of De Vries on top of the front gable. The building is now used as a museum and contains many interesting artifacts of the colonial period.

The *Holt House* was built about 1685 and first served as an inn. Ryves Holt moved to Lewes in 1721 from Philadelphia and became naval officer of the port and sheriff of Sussex County. In December of 1750 he went with John Watson, the Penns' surveyor, to Fenwick's Island to begin the survey of the boundary between Delaware and Maryland.

Milford

The *Causey Mansion* was built in 1763 by an English architect named Mitchell for Levin Crapper, a landowner whose fifteen hundred acres included what is now South Milford. The mansion was remodeled in 1855 by Governor Peter F. Causey.

New Castle

The original *Public Square*, laid out during the time Peter Stuyvesant governed the colony, is now the Green. During the English period a log blockhouse was built, and the square was enclosed with a stockade to protect the citizens in case of attack.

On the Green still stands the *Old Court House* where the government of the Three Lower Counties was carried on until Dover was made the capital of the state in 1777. The central section, built of Flemish-bond brickwork with glazed headers in early Georgian colonial style, was the original part of the structure. It had a large gambrel roof, which was replaced by the present one after a fire in 1771. Additions have been made over two centuries.

Building was begun on *Immanuel Church and Churchyard* in 1703, but the structure was later completely remodeled. A few of the gravestones in the churchyard are dated as early as 1707.

The *Old Presbyterian Church* replaced in 1707 the earliest church building in New Castle, a small wooden church built by the Swedes and Dutch and dedicated in 1657.

The *Amstel House*, now the home of the New Castle Historical Society, is thought to have been built about 1730. It is believed that the present kitchen wing was the residence in 1706 when the first recorded transfer was made. No two windows in the house are exactly alike, although two are placed symmetrically on either side of the door.

The *Van Leuvenigh House*, built in 1732, was the home of Zachariah Van Leuvenigh, chief magistrate of New Castle during the Revolution. Postriders of the Committee of Correspondence brought the news of the battles of Lexington and Bunker Hill to Van Leuvenigh here, where he signed the messages and bade the riders godspeed to Baltimore.

Newark

Although the first *Academy* building, erected in 1776 from funds raised partly in England, has long since been torn down, the town library occupies one of the buildings of the later Academy of Newark. Inscriptions in old books show that Newark had a library as early as 1763.

About three miles from Newark is *Cooch's Bridge* and old *Cooch House*. A monument marks the spot where the only battle of the Revolution on Delaware soil took place and where the Stars and Stripes was first unfurled in action.

Pilot Town (about one mile northwest of Lewes)

A granite block marks the spot believed to be the site of the fort built by the Dutch when they landed at Zwaanendael in 1631. An inscription by George Bancroft reads: "That Delaware exists as a separate Commonwealth is due to this colony."

Rehoboth

The *Homestead* was built about 1742 by Peter Marsh, who settled here to be near the pirate gold he thought was buried in the dunes nearby. The house was carefully restored by Colonel W. S. Corkran many years later and used for his home.

Wilmington

Old Swedes (Holy Trinity) *Church* was built as Swedish Lutheran but is now Protestant Episcopal. It was built in 1698 under the direction of the Reverend Eric Bjorck. Beneath the brick pavement and under the walls of the church are buried the remains of many early settlers. To the south of the altar is buried Petter Bjorck, died September 20, 1710, son of Eric Bjorck. Mary Vining is said to be buried in the churchyard in an unmarked grave, and the tomb of Major Peter Jaquett bears a lengthy inscription of his service in the Revolutionary War.

The Rocks, site of Fort Christina and the landing of the Swedes, is now a state park, where a stone monument marks the place where Peter Minuit landed in late March 1638 and built Fort Christina, named for the young queen of Sweden, and established the first permanent settlement of Europeans in Delaware.

Rodney Square, in the heart of Wilmington, is surrounded by modern buildings of administration, finance, and business. On the Market Street side stands the statue of Caesar Rodney on horseback, designed by James Kelly of New York. It honors the signer of the Declaration of Independence for whom the square is named.

The Colonial Dames now use the small Dutch colonial red-brick building which was built in 1740 as the *First Presbyterian Church* for their meeting place.

What is thought to be the site of the *Old Barley Mill* is marked by a large flat millstone near the little iron and cement bridge crossing the raceway at Park Drive and Adams Street. Dr. Tymen Stidham came with the Swedish Governor Rising in 1654 and is believed to have built the first Brandywine mill for cleaning barley here.

Old Brandywine Ford near the foot of Adams Street was used by travelers before 1764. Elizabeth Shipley rode across this ford in the early 1730's, and as she ascended the hill beyond it, she saw the scene of a dream in which a guide had told her that she and her family should move here. When she finally persuaded her husband to visit the spot, he saw the potential of power in the Brandywine and moved there, where he prospered greatly.

Washington's Headquarters just before the Battle of the Brandywine was a two-story house at what is now 303 West Street. It was chosen because of its high location, and Washington stayed there from August 25, 1777, until September 8, when he marched with his troops to Chadd's Ford to fight the English.

Index